STROKEWORK FLOWERS
Step by Step

DECORATIVE PAINTING

STROKEWORK FLOWERS
Step by Step

MARGOT
CLARK

NORTH LIGHT BOOKS
CINCINNATI, OHIO
www.nlbooks.com

ABOUT THE AUTHOR

My earliest artistic recollection is of drawing paper dolls for my fourth grade class and having the teacher draw them clothes. Wasn't she a saint! I have always loved to draw, paint and make things with my hands, especially when they actually serve a purpose. I enjoy decorating my home, gardening and absolutely adore flowers. When I discovered Decorative Art and learned it was a true art form I was overjoyed. This was what I had been searching for all those years. I then joined the Society of Decorative Painters and my life changed forever. I took classes, began to teach, owned a retail store - realized I loved teaching and designing but did not enjoy running a store, went to work for a color company, began writing magazine articles and pattern packets and just continued on from there. I have taught throughout the United States, Bermuda, Italy, Canada and Sweden. I consider myself very lucky to be able to make my living being involved in the Decorative Art industry.

Strokework Flowers Step by Step. Copyright © 2000 by Margot Clark. Manufactured in China. All rights reserved. The patterns and drawings in this book are for the personal use of the decorative painter. By permission of the author and publisher, they may be either hand-traced or photocopied to make single copies, but under no circumstances may they be resold or republished. It is permissible for the purchaser to paint the designs contained herein and sell them at fairs, bazaars and craft shows. No other part of this book may be reproduced in any form or by any electronic or mechanical means including information storage and retrieval systems without permission in writing from the publisher, except by a reviewer, who may quote brief passages in a review. Published by North Light Books, an imprint of F&W Publications, Inc., 1507 Dana Avenue, Cincinnati, Ohio 45207. (800) 289-0963. First edition.

Other fine North Light Books are available from your local bookstore, art supply store or direct from the publisher.

04 03 02 01 00   5 4 3 2 1

Library of Congress Cataloging-in-Publication Data

Clark, Margot
    Strokework Flowers Step by Step/ Margot Clark.
        p.   cm.
    ISBN 0-89134-926-X (pb: alk. paper)
    1. Painting 2. Decoration and ornament 3. Flowers in art. I. Title
TT385.C57 2000
745.7'23-dc21

Editors: Heather Dakota and Kathy Kipp
Designer: Mary Barnes Clark
Production Artist: Kathy Gardner
Production Coordinator: Kristen D. Heller
Photographer: Christine Polomsky

DEDICATION

This book is dedicated to my husband, Harold, my daughters Jaime and Jennifer and my sisters, Martha and Tina. They have always believed in me, encouraged me to aim higher and higher and been proud of me. It meant the difference between success and failure. Thank you.

ACKNOWLEDGMENTS

I would like to thank Melinda Neist who taught me the traditional style of multi-loading and encouraged me to develop my Contemporary Multi-load Floral Technique. Thanks, also, to Greg Albert who discovered me, Heather Dakota and Kathy Kipp who kept me on track while writing this book, Christine Polomsky for all the wonderful photos in the book, my friends Patte Kayne, Jeanie Ireland, Karan Lamoreaux, Nancy Rustad and Kit Stoner who just listened when I needed to talk, and especially Donna Bryant Waterson, my mentor.

INTRODUCTION

When I sat down to write this introduction my mind went blank! After giving it some thought I decided to just chat and share bits of information on the Contemporary Multi-load Technique that I have developed over the years.

Like most people I have a limited amount of time and a great deal that has to be done. I love strokework but also want a lot of depth to the strokes. Multi-loading allows me to have both in a short period of time. I learned the traditional method of multi-loading and then worked on adapting the technique to more contemporary flowers, colors and designs. I still use one round sable brush, Margot's Multi-load, for almost all of my work but like to add a bit more shading, if necessary, with an angle shader. I call this style of painting "controlled freedom." After learning how to control the brush and the construction of the flowers, you have the freedom to paint them anywhere, on anything at any time you choose. Part of my goal in writing this book is to give you, the reader, the ability to look past the projects and be able to paint the flowers in the book on any surface - walls included - without needing a pattern. The patterns in this book are just guides. Move the flowers around and interchange them between patterns if you like. Practice painting them so you can paint with just a general outline to follow. As you practice the flowers in this book, really watch the endings to your strokes. If you allow them to cross over where they do not belong you will lose the illusion of a petal or a leaf on the surface and then it will just look like paint.

My inspiration comes from many sources. A beautiful surface is inspiring, so is the challenge of incorporating an idea into a decorated room and having it all work. A new product is exciting also. Flowers are my favorite subject matter and just wandering in my garden or the local garden center is enough to make me grab my camera or sketchpad.

One last thing before going on to paint. I keep talking about practice. Well, look in the middle of the word practice—there is the word act. Also, the first two letters and the last three letters spell price. So, the price you pay for acting on the word practice is excellence. I will leave you with that thought.

Margot

CHAPTER

1

MATERIALS

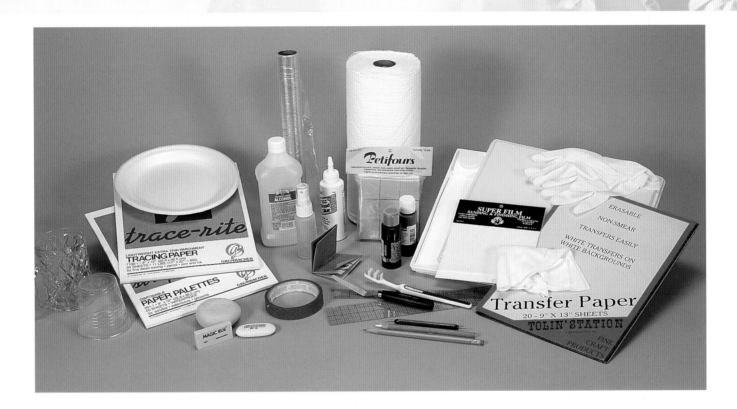

GENERAL SUPPLIES

Pad of Paper Palettes for Acrylics
I use these for basecoating colors or
when a product needs to be kept
drier than on a wet palette.

Foam Plate I use this for my palette
when using the Chemtek Metallic
Finishes.

Sta-Wet Palette by Masterson is
essential for the thin shading technique. Keep the sponge full of water.
Wet the palette paper until it's
translucent. Both sides of the palette
paper can be used.

Glass Water Container is used to
wash the brush at the end of the
painting session and clean the brush
between color loads. To prepare the
brush for painting, I wet it, press it
against the side of the container and
go directly to the paint. This
method keeps both the bristles and
the paint moist.

Transfer Paper I keep both gray
and white graphite transfer paper in
my painting supplies for use on light
and dark surfaces.

Tracing Paper Use the tracing to
transfer the design and protect the

original. You can see through the
tracing paper to check for proper
placement of the design as you
transfer.

Rubbing Alcohol Used to create
the faux tortoiseshell finish on
the "Garden of Roses Sewing Box"
project.

Spritzer Bottle The rubbing alcohol
is spritzed on the wet liquid metals
and patinas.

Plastic Wrap Used to create the
faux burled walnut on the "Garden
of Roses Sewing Box" project.

Wood Glue A must when you need to make a repair or attach something.

Sandpaper I use medium and fine grades to sand wood in the direction of the wood grain prior to sealing with wood sealer.

PRODUCTS TO CREATE SPECIAL FINISHES

Chemtek products are real, nontoxic liquid metals that actually oxidize using environmentally safe chemicals to create patinaed finishes. All products are water-based.

• **Aqueous Sealer** Used first under the technique as a primer coat and after the technique as a protectant for the patinaed finish.

• **Metallic Finishes** In this book I have used Gold, Copper, Brass and Dark Bronze. They are actual crushed metal flakes in an acrylic base.

• **Patinas** I have used two: Green Patina on the "Pansies on Glass" project and Aqua Blue Patina on the "Angel-wing Roses Table" project. These products actually oxidize the liquid metals.

• **Insta-Neutralizer** This anti-oxidizing agent halts the oxidation process immediately.

• **Two Step Fine Crackle Finish** by Delta creates a crackle finish.

PREPPING, FINISHING AND BRUSH CLEANING PRODUCTS

• **J.W. Etc. Brush Cleaner** for cleaning brushes.
• **J.W. Etc. Wood Filler** for filling in holes and covering imperfections in your wood.
• **J.W. Etc. First Step Wood Sealer** Used to seal wood after sanding and before basecoating.
• **J.W. Etc. Right Step Satin Varnish** Brush-on varnish.
• **J.W. Etc. Right Step Gloss Varnish** Brush-on varnish.

• **J.W. Etc. Finishing Wax** Used for final coating after varnish has dried.
• **Etchall Dip 'n Etch Liquid** Used to etch glass. Reusable.
• **Spray Varnishes** I use both Delta and DecoArt brands. I like to use these when I have large areas to cover or small pieces that are hard to hold.

MARGOT'S MULTI-LOAD BRUSH
All multi-load painting is done with this brush. It is a top-quality sable hair brush manufactured by Eagle Brush according to my specifications.

OTHER BRUSHES
The rest of the brushes I use are all synthetic brushes by Eagle Brush. I like the Millenium Series best, followed by the Azure Series.

Millenium Series:
- **755 no. 1 Mini-Liner** used for tendrils and leaf veins.
- **750 no. 1 Script Liner** longer bristles, also used for tendrils.
- **710 ½-inch (12mm) Angle Shader** used for all floated color techniques.
- **715 no. 14 Flat Shader**, **770 ¾-inch (19mm) Flat Wash/Glaze**, used for basecoating, applying washes of color and varnishing.

- **Azure Series 570 1-inch (25mm) Flat Wash /Glaze** It is advisable to designate one brush strictly for varnishing so it does not become contaminated by dried paint or other products.

CARING FOR YOUR BRUSHES

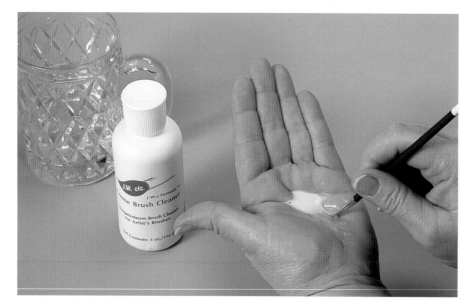

CLEAN YOUR BRUSH

Your brushes will last much longer if you care for them properly. Rinse the excess paint from the bristles by swishing the brush in the water container. Place the brush cleaner in the palm of your hand and drag the bristles through the cleaner pressing against the palm of your hand making sure the cleaner gets up to the ferrule.

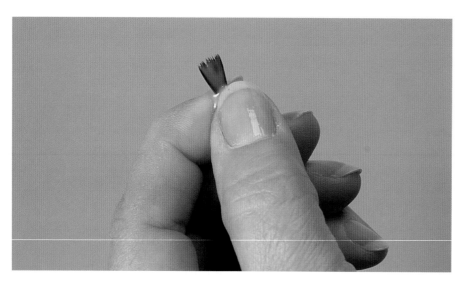

CLEAN AROUND THE FERRULE

Since the brush is not washed out during use except when changing colors, it is important to take special care in cleaning around the ferrule to remove any build-up of paint. Pinch around the ferrule with your finger and thumb to loosen any paint that has worked its way up that far.

TAP THE FERRULE

Tap the ferrule against the side of the glass container to clean. Never drag the bristles across the bottom of any container or you will get split ends on the brush hairs. I clean my synthetic brushes this way also. Give them all one final rinse under cool tap water, pinch out the excess moisture, reshape them with your fingers and lay them on their sides to dry.

CHAPTER

TERMS & TECHNIQUES 2

PREPARE THE SURFACE

Fill any holes or indentations with wood filler and a palette knife. Sand the wood smooth with medium sandpaper, then sand again with fine sandpaper. Always sand with the wood grain. Apply one coat of wood sealer. Let this dry twenty-four hours. Finally, sand again with a crumpled brown paper bag to remove the raised wood grain caused by the wood sealer.

TRANSFER THE PATTERN

Place the design tracing on the surface, moving it around until it is where you would like it. Hold the tracing down with one hand and slide the graphite paper, transfer side down, under the tracing. Use a stylus or ball point pen to transfer the design to the surface. A pencil gets dull too quickly and widens the tracing lines.

How to Multi-load Your Brush

Fully Load the Brush

Pull the color out from the paint puddle and press the bristles against the palette, flattening the brush. Turn the brush over and load the other side and again press the bristles against the palette. This forces paint into the bristles so the paint can be carried to the end of the stroke. You should be able to see the bristles through the paint when the brush is properly loaded. If you can't see the bristles, you have too much paint on the brush.

Pull-through Color

On one side of the brush, pull a little paint out from the paint puddle. Pull the brush through loading the brush fully on one side, leaving a smear of paint on the brush.

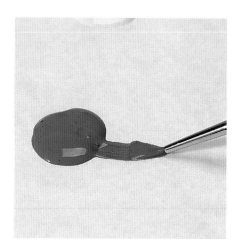 

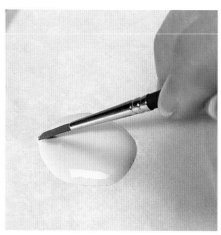 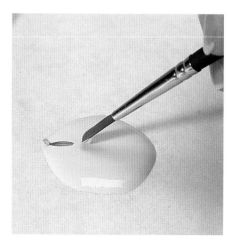 

Pick-up Color

On the opposite side of the paint puddle, touch one side of the brush down to the paint. Then pull and lift the brush up towards you, leaving a blob of paint on one side of the brush tip. The paint should extend about halfway down the bristles.

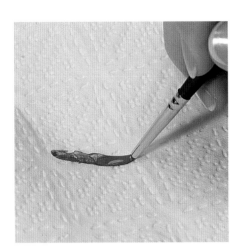

WIPE THE BRUSH

When directed to wipe the brush, do so on a damp paper towel. Usually, you'll be removing the top color and want the rest of the colors to remain on the brush. Gently wipe across the paper towel so you don't remove all the paint. Do not wash the brush in water.

CORRECT HAND POSITION

The handle of the brush is angled back with the bristles extended and your little finger should be tucked into the palm of your hand.

CORRECT HAND MOVEMENT

Lift the brush using only your fingers and wrist. Your wrist should be relaxed.

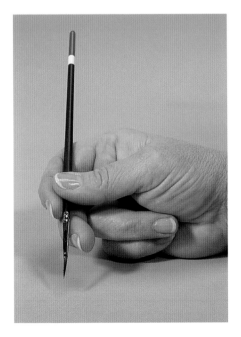

CORRECT HAND POSITION—DRIBBLE

Hold the brush horizontal to help create the dribble. Here the handle is towards the right. It could also be towards the left if that is where you want the dribble to go. Begin to push the paint on one side of the brush off the tip instead of pushing it off the side where it was loaded.

INCORRECT HAND POSITION

Lifting the brush and completing the strokes should be comfortable. As you can see here, my wrist is anything but comfortable. My little finger is sticking out and my wrist looks like I'm trying to retract my whole hand into my arm. Relax and pull back with the hand and lift up with the fingers as shown left.

BRUSHSTROKES

This Contemporary Multi-load Floral Technique is based on brushstrokes, but most of the strokes are not visible in the final painting. Instead you see beautiful, blended flowers that look like they took a long time to create. Pulling the strokes in different directions will give you control over the brush. The following strokes will teach you brush control and brush action. You'll need to learn brush action, not necessarily to paint perfect brushstrokes. Think of the strokes as tools to allow you to paint the flowers in this book.

I call this technique "controlled freedom" because learning brush control gives you the freedom to paint quickly and freely, but with precision. This technique is still a type of folk art but on a contemporary level instead of the folk art that was done hundreds of years ago. The flowers and leaves are more realistic. The designs are not so cluttered and the backgrounds are lighter.

In the explanation under the photos of the strokes I stress not to turn the brush. This means not to let it roll in your fingers unless directed to do so. You can direct the brush anywhere you like, but if it rolls you will lose control. Load the brush fully in paint, almost to the ferrule, by pulling paint out and away from the paint puddle and pressing the brush against the palette on one side then the other.

PRESS, LIFT AND CUT STROKE

LEFT SIDE—PRESS
Set the brush down with bristles at a 45-degree angle. Apply gentle pressure by pressing on the brush handle to open the bristles. Do not wiggle the brush open. Do not turn the brush.

LEFT SIDE—LIFT
Without turning the brush, lift up to the longest hairs with your fingers and wrist. Bristles will straighten out by themselves forming a straight knife/chisel edge.

LEFT SIDE—CUT
Cut straight down, creating the tail, using the chisel formed in the previous step. Keep tails straight and long. This is where you'll need your brush control.

> **HINT**
> Hold the brush just behind the ferrule and allow the brush handle to move away from you as the bristles come towards you. Keep your forearm on the table and move only your wrist and fingers as you paint these strokes. Tuck your little finger inside the palm of your hand.

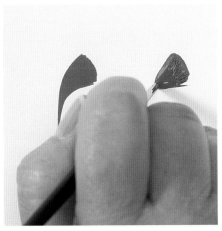

RIGHT SIDE—PRESS

Again, set the brush down with bristles at a 45-degree angle. Apply pressure to the brush handle to open the bristles. Do not wiggle the brush open. Do not turn the brush.

RIGHT SIDE—LIFT

Don't worry about being right- or left-handed. Everyone will need to pull strokes from the right and left. Make sure chisel edge is straight up and down before you pull to the right.

RIGHT SIDE—CUT

Be sure you're painting on the longest hairs before pulling the tail straight down. Do not turn the brush.

PRESS, LIFT, TURN AND CUT STROKE

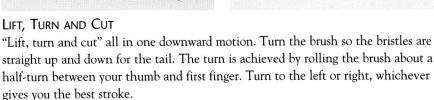

PRESS

Press the bristles open straight across for this stroke.

LIFT, TURN AND CUT

"Lift, turn and cut" all in one downward motion. Turn the brush so the bristles are straight up and down for the tail. The turn is achieved by rolling the brush about a half-turn between your thumb and first finger. Turn to the left or right, whichever gives you the best stroke.

1 TOP-HALF LEFT LEAF STROKE

These photos show both halves of a whole leaf, but they can also be used alone as filler leaves. Use the "Press, Lift and Cut" stroke shown on pages 16-17. Start on the knife edge. Slide down a bit and exert pressure on the bristles pushing them up and at a slight angle. Do not turn the brush. Then lift and cut to create the tail.

2 BOTTOM-HALF LEFT LEAF STROKE

Use the "Press, Lift and Cut" stroke for filler or shadow leaves. Start on the chisel edge. Slide down a bit and pull across exerting pressure on the bristles. Push down and at a slight angle. Release the pressure and cut in the tail. This is done in one motion without turning the brush.

3 WHOLE LEFT LEAF WITH COMBINED STROKES

Paint the top and bottom halves of the two leaf strokes again, but this time paint the top half first. Paint the beginning of the bottom half, but cut into the existing tail of the first stroke.

1 TOP-HALF RIGHT LEAF STROKE

Leading off from the right, use the same "Press, Lift and Cut" stroke as for the left side. Start on the knife edge, slide down, press open exerting pressure, forcing bristles up at an angle. Then, release pressure and cut in the tail. Do not turn the brush.

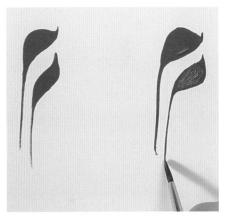

2 BOTTOM-HALF RIGHT LEAF STROKE

Begin on chisel edge, slide down, pull across exerting a little pressure to push the bristles down and at an angle. Release pressure and cut in the tail. Do not turn the brush.

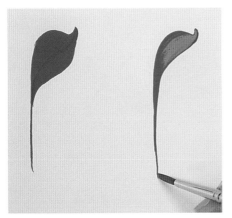

3 WHOLE RIGHT LEAF STROKE WITH COMBINED STROKES

Paint the top half first using the "Press, Lift and Cut" stroke as in steps 1 and 2. Then paint the beginning of the bottom half, cutting the tail into the previous stroke. Do not turn the brush.

DESCENDING STROKES

The two large strokes are the left and right "Press, Lift and Cut" strokes. The idea is to paint them smaller and smaller until they disappear without moving your hand or arm position. Exert less and less pressure on the bristles until you are completely off the surface. Do this on the left and right side. Then when you see tiny leaves and commas in the designs, you know they are just smaller versions of the press, lift and cut strokes. Direct the tails of these strokes as though they will eventually cut into the tail of the large stroke.

Dribble, Catch and Pull Stroke

1 DRIBBLE
This stroke deposits small blobs of excess paint to catch and pull into the design. The brush in the photo is fully loaded in red and has a pick-up of blue. Hold the brush with the blue facing away from you. Barely touch the surface and push the blue out with the tip of the bristles leaving little blobs of paint. Left-handed people should practice this stroke from right to left.

2 RELEASE PRESSURE
Release pressure and keep brush moving. Don't let the brush roll in your fingers.

3 PRESS AND RELEASE
Continue the press-and-release motion, exerting a little or a lot of pressure for the size blob you want. Keep it moving with no turns. If the pushes are close together, the form is ruffled. If they are far apart, the form is wavy.

4 CATCH THE DRIBBLE
Set the brush down just under the dribble with the dribble color facing up. Press the bristles open.

5 PUSH INTO THE DRIBBLE
Push the bristles away from you and into the paint, not against the surface. Push past the dribble for a loose, ragged edge. Push into the dribble, but not beyond it, for a smoother edge.

6 PULL
Begin to lift as you pull the dribble down and cut towards the calyx.

7 COMPLETED STROKE
Work across the dribble catching and pulling towards the calyx to complete a petal.

LONG LEAF STROKE

1 LOAD THE BRUSH
Load the brush in Gamal Green, pull through Antique Gold Deep and pick up Eggshell. Face the Eggshell side of the brush left. When you begin to paint these leaves, face the lightest color towards the light source.

2 BEGIN THE LEAF
Touch the paint to the surface with the Eggshell facing left. Only the paint should be touching. Exert pressure on the left side. Don't let the brush roll in your fingers. Keep the brush moving at all times, so the stroke flows.

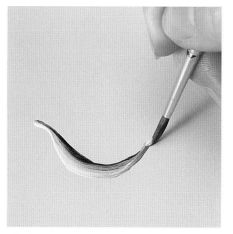

3 RELEASE PRESSURE AND LIFT
Begin to release pressure and lift the brush so the bristles are just barely touching the surface.

4 PUSH TO THE RIGHT
Now exert pressure to the right sending the Eggshell to the right. Do not turn the brush.

5 RELEASE PRESSURE
Release the pressure. Then, push the bristles to the left, exerting pressure.

6 COMPLETE THE STROKE
Lift to a point to complete the leaf. The stroke for this leaf is—touch, push to the left, lift, push to the right, lift, push to the left and lift off.

Turnback Stroke

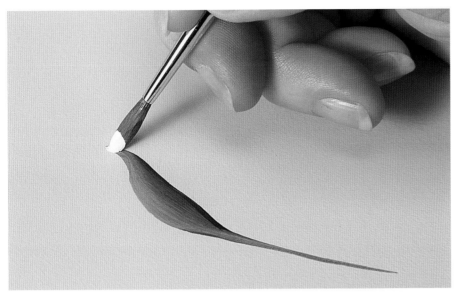

1 Paint the Leaf
Paint the leaf stroke with a load in Gamal Green, pull through Antique Gold Deep, pull through Eggshell on the same side of the brush. This is the light side of the brush, when you need to reload.Push the light side of the brush up when painting the leaf. The dark area on that leaf is also the straightest area and the perfect place for a turnback. Wipe off the light side gently, reload the dark side, really flattening the brush, and pick up a small amount of Eggshell on the light side.

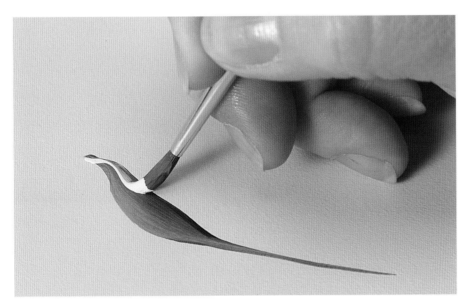

2 Paint the Turnback
Begin at the outer tip of the leaf. Face the Eggshell towards the leaf, barely touch down forming the tip of the leaf, lift, push Eggshell towards the leaf.

3 Paint the Turnback
Lift and cut in along the edge of the leaf releasing pressure until brush lifts off the surface.

Hint
This same technique applies to turnbacks and turndowns. Turnbacks face in and turndowns face out.

PROJECT

MUM, TULIPS AND DAISIES

I love boxes. They look great as decorations and make useful, wonderful gifts. Best of all, they are fun to paint. What more can you ask of a painting surface?

As you learn the multi-load technique, you will need to practice. If you practice on a real surface, as opposed to just practicing on paper, you will find that you strive for better results and will learn faster. Keep a supply of different-sized, different-colored, basecoated boxes handy. When you need a quick gift, practice your multi-load flowers, the whole design or just one or two flowers, on a box. You'll have accomplished two things at once! Painting in the multi-load technique is fast, but you need practice to become proficient.

PAINT: (D) = DELTA CERAMCOAT ACRYLICS; (DA) = DECOART AMERICANA ACRYLICS

 Magnolia White (D)

 Raw Linen (D)

 Antique Gold Deep (DA)

 Raw Sienna (DA)

 Opaque Red (D)

 Dolphin Grey (D)

 Stonewedge Green (D)

 Timberline Green (D)

 Dark Forest Green (D)

 Walnut (D)

SURFACE
• Oval wooden box; 9¼"x7" available at art/craft stores or through mail-order catalogs.

BRUSHES
• Margot's Multi-load
• 1-inch(25mm) flat wash/glaze
• no. 14 flat shader

ADDITIONAL SUPPLIES
• Fine sandpaper
• Crumpled brown paper bag
• Damp cloth
• Tracing paper
• Stylus
• Gray graphite paper
• J.W. Etc. First Step Wood Sealer

This pattern may be hand-traced or photocopied for personal use only. Enlarge at 137% to bring it up to full size. Do not transfer the numbers.

PREPARE THE SURFACE

1 BASECOAT THE BOX
Sand the box with fine sandpaper and wipe off the sanding dust with a damp cloth. Using the 1-inch (25mm) flat wash/glaze brush, apply one coat of wood sealer. Let this dry. Sand again with a crumpled brown paper bag to remove the raised wood grain.

Leave a little water in your brush as you pick up Timberline Green for basecoating the lid and base. Use two thinned coats instead of one heavy coat, providing a smooth basecoat. Use the 1-inch (25mm) flat wash/glaze brush for all basecoating except the rim of the lid; use the no. 14 flat shader loaded with Dark Forest Green in this area. Let the basecoat dry twenty-four hours. If you apply the design to a surface that isn't thoroughly dry, it is almost impossible to remove the graphite lines.

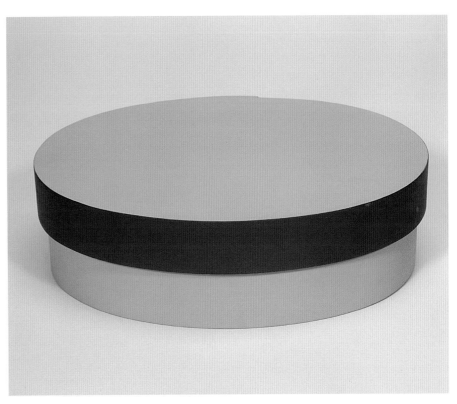

2 TRACE THE PATTERN
Trace the design on a sheet of tracing paper, omitting the tiny filler leaves. These are freehanded later.

3 TRANSFER THE PATTERN
Place the tracing on the box lid in the proper position, hold it in place with one hand and slide the gray graphite under the design. Be sure you have the graphite paper transfer side down. Use the stylus to lightly transfer the design to the box lid.

PAINT THE TULIP STEMS

1 LOAD THE BRUSH
Using Margot's Multi-load brush, fully load both sides of the brush in Dark Forest Green, flattening the brush as you load. Pull one side through Stonewedge Green picking up a smear. This is now the light side of the brush whenever you need to reload.

To reload, wipe the light side of the brush on a damp paper towel, turn the brush over to the dark side and pull the dark side through Dark Forest Green, turn it back over and pull the light side through Stonewedge Green. This method of reloading keeps the colors from blending on the palette.

2 PULL IN THE STEMS
Face the light side of the brush to the right. Add pressure to open up the bristles just enough to fill the width of the stem. Keep the same pressure and pull the stem.

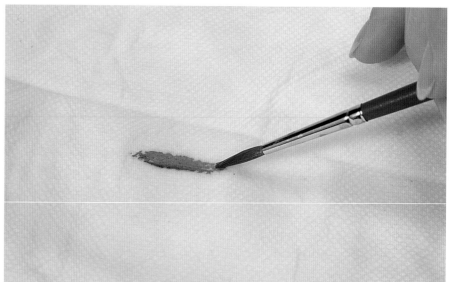

3 FINISH THE STEM
At the end, quickly lift the brush to give a nice cut end to the stem. Do the pink tulip stem first. Once this has dried, paint the yellow tulip stem across the pink tulip stem.

PAINT THE TULIP LEAVES

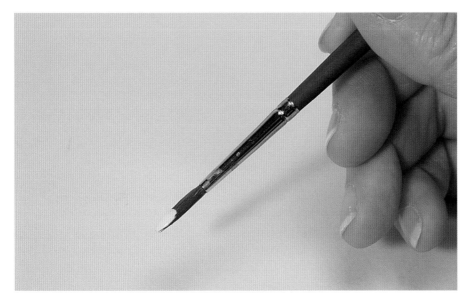

1 LOAD THE BRUSH
Reload the brush in Dark Forest Green, pull through Stonewedge Green and pick up Raw Linen on the Stonewedge Green side.

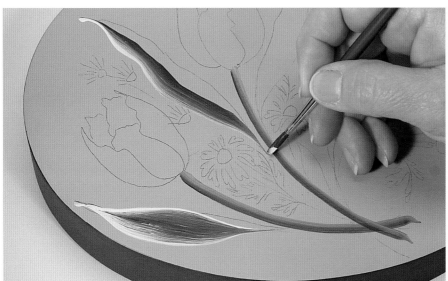

2 THE FIRST HALF OF THE LEAF
Begin at the outer leaf tip with Raw Linen facing the outer edge of the leaf. Add a little pressure, pushing Raw Linen to the outer edge, increase the pressure to fill half of the leaf and release the pressure before you reach the stem.

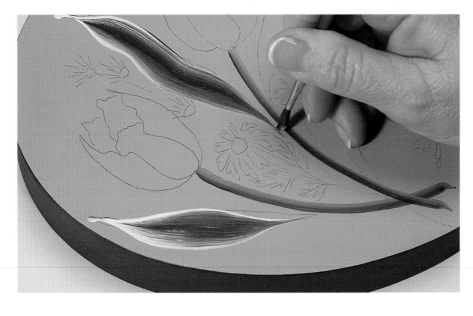

3 THE SECOND HALF OF THE LEAF
Repeat the above steps for the other half of the leaf. Again, push the Raw Linen side of the brush to the outer edge of the leaf. Complete all the tulip leaves in the same manner. Wash your brush.

PAINT THE TULIPS

1 "BREAK THE RED" AND LOAD THE BRUSH
Brush mix Walnut into Opaque Red to "break the red."
This mix will be referred to as red for the remainder of this
project. Add Raw Sienna and Magnolia White to the palette.
Fully load the brush in red, pull through Raw Sienna, just a
smear, and pick up the Magnolia White on the Raw Sienna
side.

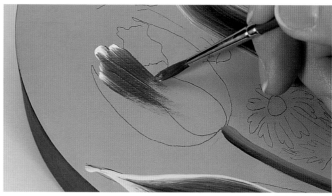

2 PAINT THE FIRST PETAL
Paint the tulip on the left first. Hold the brush with the
white facing out. With the tip of the brush, dribble across the
back of the petal leaving a ridge of paint. Wipe off the excess
white on a damp paper towel. Turn and set the brush with the
white side facing up under the dribble. Apply a little pressure,
catch the dribble and pull down toward the calyx.

3 TRIPLE LOAD YOUR BRUSH
with Red, Raw Sienna and Magnolia White. Dribble the
white as you did previously. Catch it and pull it toward the

calyx. Repeat the catch and pull until the petal is filled in.
Repeat for petals two, three and the front petal.

4 PAINT THE TULIP SIDE PETALS
Begin to dribble the petal by touching down the white,
facing towards the inside of the tulip. Lift and dribble across

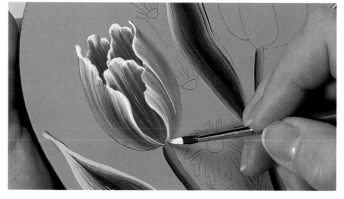

the number three petal. Repeat the same steps from the first
petal. Repeat this step for the other side. Wash the brush.

PAINT THE YELLOW TULIP

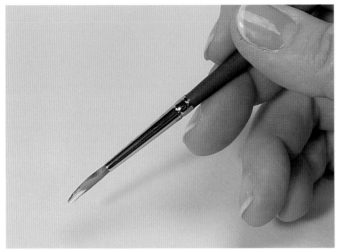

1 LOAD THE BRUSH
Load both sides of the brush in Antique Gold Deep. Pull one side lightly through the red mix, turn the brush over and pick up white on the gold side. Don't reload the red unless necessary or the flower will look orange. This load will give a yellow flower with just a blush of red.

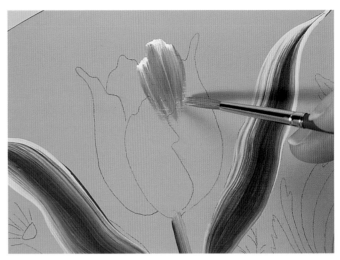

2 PAINT THE YELLOW TULIP PETALS
Dribble, Wipe, Catch and Pull just as you did for the pink tulip.

3 PAINT THE YELLOW MIDDLE PETAL
With white facing the top of the tulip, dribble white across the top of the petal. Turn the white of the brush to the left and connect it with the left edge of the dribble, pushing the white out to the left. Wipe off the excess white, catch and pull the dribble to the calyx, rounding out the sides of the petal as you pull the stroke.

4 PAINT THE YELLOW TULIP SIDE PETAL
Dribble white, cut to calyx, catch and pull. Remember to go in at the waist of the tulip and out at the hips forming the tulip shape. Wash the brush.

PAINT THE MUM STEMS & LEAVES

1 PAINT THE STEMS
Load Margot's Multi-load brush with Dark Forest Green and pull through Stonewedge Green. Pull all the stems beginning with the light side of the brush facing the top of the design.

2 PAINT THE MUM LEAVES
Reload in both greens, check to see which is the light side and pick up Magnolia White. Work one section at a time with the white facing the outer edge of the leaf, and push white to the tips of the top section. This will leave little blobs of white paint.

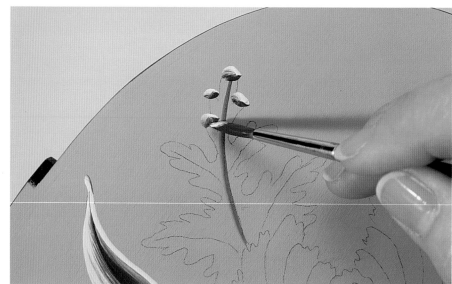

3 FILL IN THE MUM LEAVES
Turn the white side of the brush up, gently grab the white blob of paint and pull it towards the center vein line, filling in the top section of the leaf. Repeat for each section and all mum leaves. Wash the brush.

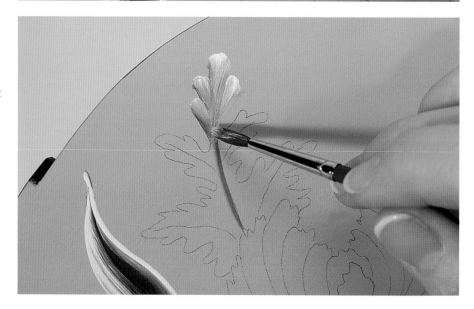

PAINT THE MUM

1 PAINT THE FIRST TWO MUM PETALS
Load both sides of the brush in the red mix, and pull one side through Antique Gold Deep. Then, pick up Magnolia White on the gold side. Dribble two or three times at the outer tip of the petal, catch the dribble and pull it into the calyx. Refer to the pattern on page 26 for the sequence of the petals.

2 PAINT MUM PETALS NOS. 3-10
Follow the numerical sequence on the pattern for petals 3-10. Place strokes right next to each other and don't allow them to cross over one another.

3 PAINT THE NO. 11 MUM PETAL
Pick up white, dribble across the top of the petal. Push white to the right and then to the left. Turn the white side of the brush up, catch the dribble and pull the stroke into the calyx, filling in the petal.

Paint the Mum, CONTINUED

4 PAINT THE NO. 12 MUM PETAL
Pick up white and dribble it across the top of the petal. Push white to the right and then to the left. Turn the white side of the brush up, catch the dribble and pull it into the calyx, filling in the petal. Refer to the pattern on page 26 for the sequence of painting the petals.

5 PAINT THE BOTTOM MUM PETAL
Pick up white and dribble it across the top of the petal. Push white to the right and then to the left. Turn the white side of the brush up, catch the dribble and pull it into the calyx, filling in the petal.

6 PAINT THE MUM CENTER
Load the tip of the brush in Antique Gold Deep. Then, pick up a little white on one side. Face the white to the top of the design and dab in the center leaving some of the background showing through the center. Wash the brush.

PAINT THE DAISIES

1 PAINT THE DAISY STEMS
Flatten the brush in Dark Forest Green and pull one side through Magnolia White slightly blending, keeping the brush flat. Face the light side to the top or right side of the design, stay up on the knife edge of the brush and pull in all daisy stems. Wash the brush.

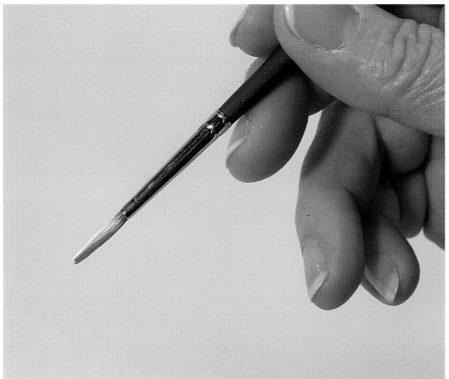

2 LOAD THE BRUSH
Load both sides with Dolphin Grey and pick up Magnolia White on one side.

PAINT THE DAISIES, CONTINUED

3 PAINT THE DAISY PETAL
Begin at the bottom center and work to the left picking up Magnolia White for each petal. This naturally shades the daisy by keeping the darkest strokes to the bottom and left side of the design. These strokes are quick "press, lift and cut" strokes.

4 THE SECOND HALF OF PETAL
The second half of the petal is done in the same manner as the first.

THE COMPLETED DAISIES

Paint the Daisy Bud

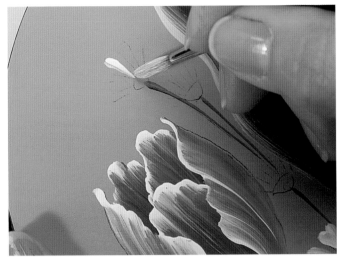

1 Paint the First Daisy Bud Petal
Reload the brush in Dolphin Grey and pick up Magnolia White. First stroke in the middle petal with Magnolia White to the right side of the petal using the "press, lift, turn and cut stroke."

2 Paint the Second Petal for the Daisy Bud
Keep the white facing right. Alternate strokes from one side to the other, starting on the outer edge of bud petals.

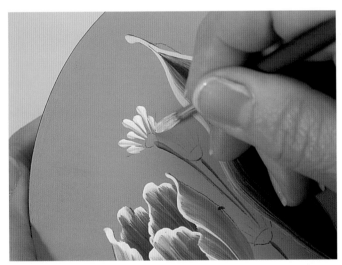

3 Final Stroke for Daisy Bud
Repeat these strokes for the rest of the daisy buds. Wash the brush.

The Completed Daisy Buds

PAINT THE DAISY CENTER

1 BASE THE CENTER
Load Antique Gold Deep, pull through the red mix. Facing the gold to the top of center and starting at the bottom of center, push gold up, forming a crown. Make your hand shake the brush nervously as you paint. Then, release pressure back at the bottom edge of the center, forming a half circle. Wipe the brush.

2 TAP IN THE WHITE
Roll the brush to a point in Magnolia White. Using the tip of the brush, lightly tap about three-quarters of the way around the bottom of the center. Tap up to the top one-third. Wipe the brush.

3 TAP IN THE WALNUT
Dip your brush tip into the Walnut paint puddle and lightly tap about three-quarters of the way around the bottom of the center. Tap on the center and the petals. Wash the brush.

PAINT THE CALYXES & LEAVES

1 PAINT THE DAISY BUD CALYXES
Fully load the brush in Dark Forest Green and pull one side through Stonewedge Green. Facing the light side towards the bud, push the Stonewedge Green up, releasing pressure to form the calyx. Wipe the light side of the brush.

2 PAINT THE DAISY LEAVES
Reload with Dark Forest Green and pull one side through Stonewedge Green, flattening as you load. Face the light side towards the top of the design and pull in the vein and stems. Fill in the leaves with "touch, lift and cut" strokes.

3 PAINT THE LARGE FILLER LEAVES
Reload the brush as in the previous stroke and face the light side towards the stem. Start on the chisel edge, slide down the chisel and pull toward the stem. Release the pressure and return to the chisel edge, cutting toward the stem.

4 PAINT THE SMALL FILLER LEAVES
Reload the dark side of the brush in Dark Forest Green and pull the light side through Timberline Green. Face the dark side to the left. The small leaves are "press, lift and cut" strokes. Refer to the pattern for placement. Wash the brush.

5 ERASE THE GRAPHITE LINES
Erase all the graphite lines. If some are caught under the paint and you can still see them, don't worry. They will just look like part of the painting.

PAINT THE BORDER

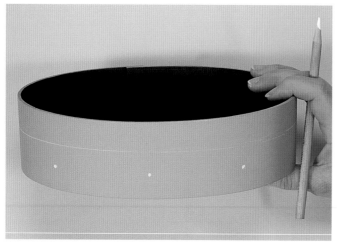

1 PLACE THE BORDER
Divide the space evenly with a chalk pencil. Allow enough room at the top for the edge of the lid to sit down over the bottom.

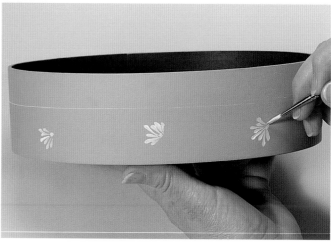

2 PAINT THE DAISY BUDS
Paint the buds the same as the ones on the lid. Refer to page 37 for detailed instructions. Paint one bud at each dot with some of the buds tipping up and others down.

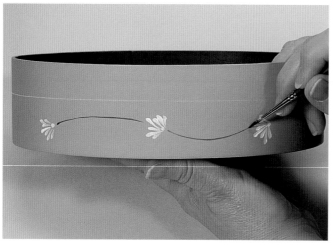

3 PAINT THE STEMS
Load the brush in Dark Forest Green, flatten and pull one side through Stonewedge Green. Face the light side towards the top of the design and pull in the stems. Alternate the curve of the stems to fit the bud placement. Allow the brush to roll in your fingers to follow the curve.

4 PAINT THE FILLER LEAVES AND CALYXES
Give the brush tip a slight push up in the calyxes and cut in the filler leaves. Refer to the pattern for placement. You can always add or take away leaves to fit the design on the box. Allow the box to dry for twenty-four hours. When it's dry use two coats of a spray satin varnish. Allow the varnish to dry overnight. To finish, apply one coat of J.W. Etc. Finishing Wax.

THE COMPLETED BOX

THE COMPLETED BOX BOTTOM

THE COMPLETED LID

GERANIUMS ON DOOR GUARD

Geraniums are one of my favorite flowers. My whole kitchen is decorated with red geraniums and this door guard goes on my pantry door. What a difference it makes! Geraniums always look so crisp, fresh and colorful and the complementary color scheme of red/green assures success.

For this project try to keep all your strokes neat and tidy. Be careful when you dribble and catch the edge of a leaf or petal. Be sure to pull to the base of the leaf or the calyx of the flower.

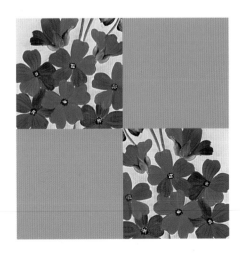

MATERIALS

PAINT: (D) = DELTA CERAMCOAT ACRYLICS; (DA) = DECOART AMERICANA ACRYLICS

Magnolia
White (D)

Raw Linen
(D)

Tangerine
(D)

Opaque Red
(D)

Dark Forest
Green (D)

Walnut
(D)

Yellow
Light (DA)

SURFACE

- Wooden door guards
  by Jim Bittner

BRUSHES

- Margot's Multi-load
- 1-inch (25mm) flat wash/glaze
  brush
- no. 14 flat shader
- ½-inch (12mm) angle shader
- no. 1 script liner

ADDITIONAL SUPPLIES

- J.W. Etc. First Step Wood Sealer
- Fine sandpaper
- Crumpled brown paper bag
- Tracing paper
- Stylus
- Gray graphite paper

TOP HALF   BOTTOM HALF

Float color around door
knob opening.

This pattern may
be hand-traced or
photocopied for
personal use only.
Enlarge to 118%
to bring it up to
full size.

Float color around door
knob opening.

KEY
x = dark red
o = red pick-up orange
no mark = dark red pick-up red

PAINT THE LEAVES AND STEMS

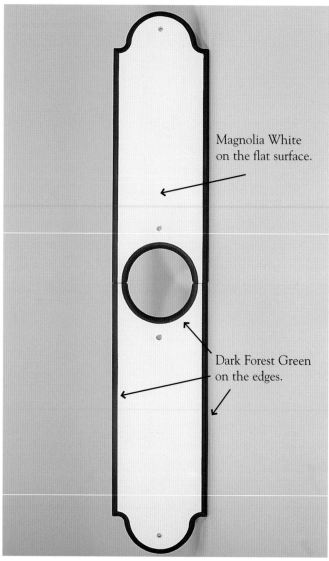

Magnolia White on the flat surface.

Dark Forest Green on the edges.

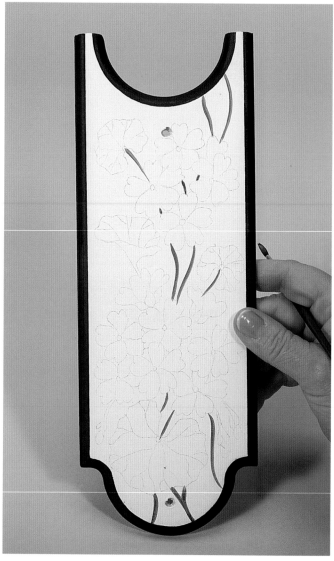

1 PREPARE THE SURFACE
Sand the surface with the wood grain. Brush on one coat of wood sealer. Sand again lightly with the brown paper bag. Basecoat the door guards with Magnolia White and Dark Forest Green. Apply the pattern. Refer to page 13 for detailed instructions on preparing the surface and applying the pattern.

2 PAINT THE STEMS
Load Margot's Multi-load brush in Dark Forest Green, pull through Magnolia White and blend slightly on the palette to create a lighter green value on the light side of the brush. Face the light side of the brush to the right or top of the design. Apply steady pressure and pull in all stems. Do not pull the stems through flower petals as the green stem will show through the red petals. Wash the brush.

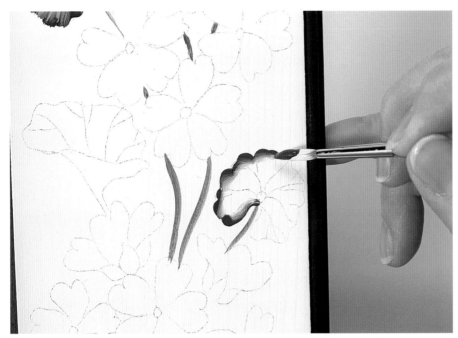

3 DRIBBLE ON THE OUTER EDGE OF THE SMALL LEAF

Load fully in Magnolia White, pick up Dark Forest Green. With Dark Forest Green facing the outer edge of the leaf, dribble halfway around the outer edge of the leaf, beginning at the stem.

4 PULL TO CENTER

Wipe off the excess green and turn the dark side of the brush to the ceiling. Set the brush down under the dribble and use the press, lift, turn and cut stroke, pulling to the stem. Repeat the dribble, catch and pull to fill in the other half of the leaf. Paint all the small leaves in this manner. Remember to paint half of the leaf at a time or the dribble will dry before you can get back to catch it.

PAINT THE LEAVES AND STEMS, CONTINUED

5 PAINT THE LARGE LEAF
The large leaf is painted with the same load and same stroke as the smaller leaves, but the dribbled edge is broken up into three segments. Paint one side, the middle section and then the other side of the leaf in that order so you are painting wet-into-wet.

6 THE TURNED-BACK LEAF
Load the brush the same as for the previous leaves. Use the same stroke, pulling in toward the stem, but stop the strokes just beyond the turned edge.

7 FRONT OF TURNED-BACK LEAF
Dribble Dark Forest Green, facing the inside of the leaf, across the front of the leaf and connect the edges to the back section.

8 THE SIDE OF LEAF AND STEM
Catch the dribble and pull down to the stem. Be careful to keep the outer sides curving in toward the stem. Don't just pull them straight. The leaf won't look natural.

Paint the Geraniums

1 Paint the Darkest Geranium Petals
Brush mix Walnut into Opaque Red to get a dark, rich red. Load fully in the dark red mix and pick up the dark mix. This will give a heavier concentration of color at the outer edge of the petal.

Dribble across the top of the petal. Remove the excess red mix on a damp paper towel and catch the dribble, pulling down to the calyx in the center of the flower. Paint only the petals marked with an "x" on the pattern shown on page 45. Wipe the brush.

2 Paint the Medium-Value Petals
Load fully in the dark red mix, then pick up Opaque Red. Dribble across the top of the petal. Remove the excess Opaque Red from the brush and repeat the catch and pull. Paint all the petals that have no "x" or "o" markings on the pattern. Wipe the brush.

3 PAINT THE LIGHTEST-VALUE PETALS
Load fully in Opaque Red and pick up Tangerine. Dribble across the top of the petal and remove the excess paint from the brush. Catch and pull all the petals that are marked with an "o" on the pattern. Wipe the brush.

4 PAINT THE BUDS
Load fully in the dark red mix and pull one side of the brush gently through Tangerine. Face the Tangerine side to the ceiling. Beginning at the outer tip of the bud, use small "press, lift, turn and cut" strokes. Reload for each bud. Pull all the buds toward the stem. Wash the brush.

PAINT THE CALYXES

1 PAINT THE BUD CALYXES

Load the brush fully in Dark Forest Green, and pull through Raw Linen. Remember the buds hang upside down, so the Raw Linen side should face the right. Keep this in mind as you turn the design to paint. When you actually paint the calyxes, the light side will face the left. Paint the calyxes in small "press, lift and cut" strokes.

2 PAINT THE FIRST CALYX STROKE
Again you are painting the design upside down. Keep the light side of the brush facing the outer edges. Use the "press, lift, turn and cut" stroke. Turn your work to make painting more comfortable.

3 PAINT THE THIRD CALYX STROKE
Turn the light side of the brush to the ceiling for the middle stroke. Use the "press, lift, turn and cut" stroke just as you did before.

4 PAINT THE MIDDLE CALYX STROKE
Repeat the steps above using the same stroke for the final calyx leaf. Wash the brush.

THE FINISHING TOUCHES

1 ADD THE VEIN LINES

Freehand the vein lines using the no. 1 script liner brush. Load the liner brush in water and pull through a bit of Dark Forest Green creating an inky consistency. Roll the brush hairs to a point. Begin at the stem end of the leaf and pull thin lines to the outer edge of the leaf. Then pull lines from the previous vein lines towards the outer edge, making small branches. Shaking your hand a little while painting the vein lines will help them look more realistic.

2 PAINT THE FLOWER CENTERS

Pick up Dark Forest Green on Margot's Multi-load brush, and dab onto the center unevenly. You do not want perfect round circles! Wipe the brush and pick up Raw Linen. Make a few dots in the center staying in the middle of the Dark Forest Green area. Do not use a stylus as it gives too perfect a dot. Paint about four flower sections at a time, so the Dark Forest Green doesn't get a chance to dry. Wash the brush.

3 FLOAT THE LEAF MARKINGS
Using the ½-inch (12mm) angle shader, float the thinned dark red mix on all the leaves. The red faces toward the outer edge of leaf. Wash the brush. The large leaf gets a second shading of thinned Dark Forest Green with the color facing the inside of the leaf.

HINT
This is a glazing technique and can always be repeated if it dries too light, but it is hard to remove if it is painted too dark.

4 SHADE THE DOOR HANDLE AREA
Float thinned Dark Forest Green around the inner edge of the door guard on the top and bottom pieces, using the ½-inch (12mm) angle shader.

HINT
Keep handy a clean, damp paper towel that is wadded into a ball, and if you get too much color, tap it off with the damp paper towel.

5 SHADOWS BEHIND THE DESIGN
Side-load the ½-inch angle shader in thinned Dark Forest Green, but tap the long corner of the brush into the design behind the flower clusters and leaves, in the center of the design. This suggests that the flowers are casting a shadow onto the surface. The shading should be heaviest at the bottom of the design and fade to almost nothing at the top. Wash the brush.

THE FINISHING TOUCHES, CONTINUED

WARM UP THE DESIGN

All the red and green may make the painting cold-looking. Add a little yellow to warm it up. Make a *very thin* wash of Yellow Light. This is a very strong color, so keep it *very thin*! Remember you can always add another wash of color. Using Margot's Multi-load brush or the ½-inch (12mm) angle shader, place the Yellow Light so it radiates from the stem end at the base of the leaves.

PROTECT THE DOOR GUARDS

Apply five or six coats of satin varnish, allowing proper drying time between coats, about four hours. Apply a coat of J.W. Etc. Finishing Wax after the last coat of varnish has dried for twenty-four hours. I like to have my design well protected.

PROJECT

PANSIES ON GLASS

Pansies are such cheerful flowers. They come in so many different color combinations with clearly defined petals and leaves, perfect for my Contemporary Multi-load Technique. They are also a bit more detailed than the flowers learned in the previous chapters. You'll learn how to multi-load the brush with four colors to paint the yellow petals. Some new challenges!

MATERIALS

PAINT: (D) = DELTA CERAMCOAT ACRYLICS; (DA) = DECOART AMERICANA ACRYLICS

 Magnolia White (D)

 Raw Linen (D)

 Raw Sienna (D)

 Yellow Light (DA)

 Antique Gold Deep (DA)

 Gamal Green (D)

 Cranberry Wine (DA)

 Dioxazine Purple (DA)

SURFACE
- Glass Corner Panel by Cooper's Works (see List of Suppliers page 127)

BRUSHES
- Margot's Multi-load
- no. 14 flat shader

CHEMTEK PRODUCTS
- Aqueous Sealer
- Copper Metallic Finish
- Green Patina

ADDITIONAL SUPPLIES
- Etchall Dip 'n Etch Liquid
- Tracing paper
- Soft white cloth

This pattern may be hand-traced or photocopied for personal use only. Enlarge at 128% to bring it up to full size. Paint the petals in numerical order.

PREPARE THE SURFACE

The glass piece used in this project can be hung on the wall by the point or by two hooks. Then hang it in a window with a second one for a really beautiful effect.

The good thing about painting on etched glass is that the acrylic paint doesn't come off. The bad thing is that the acrylic paint doesn't come off. Be sure of your technique before beginning to paint on the glass. If you make an error, change the design! The designs and patterns in this book are merely a guide to help you learn the technique.

This is a good design to take apart and use on other surfaces. Trace each flower separately on tracing paper using a black fine-line permanent pen. Do the same for the buds and the leaves. Lay them on top of one another and move them around to create a new design. Try one pansy, a bud and a few leaves on a small box. Try different color combinations, remembering to pull through Raw Sienna before picking up white when using any red color. This will keep the colors from turning muddy and tones down the intensity.

ETCH THE GLASS

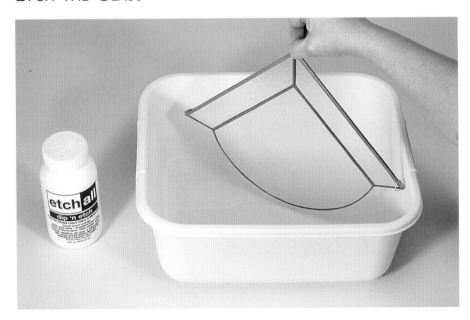

1 POUR IN THE ETCHING LIQUID
Pour etching liquid into a container big enough for the glass to lie flat. The liquid should completely cover the glass. Immerse the glass in the etching liquid for about fifteen minutes.

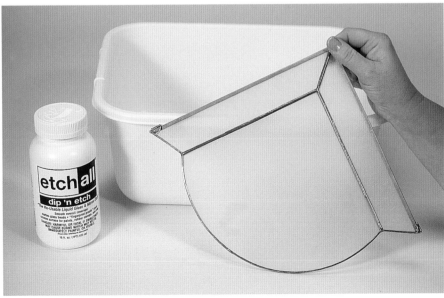

2 REMOVE THE GLASS
Remove the glass from the container and rinse the etched glass with water. Be sure to remove all the etching liquid. Return the excess liquid to its jar for future use. On this project, the etching is used to create additional tooth for your paint to adhere to the glass surface.

PREPARE THE SURFACE, CONTINUED

PATINA THE GLASS TRIM

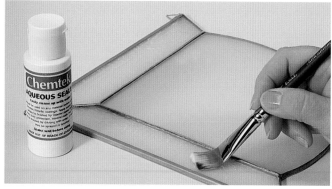

1 APPLY THE PRIMER/SEALER
Brush one coat of Aqueous Sealer onto the glass trim with a no. 14 flat shader. Let this dry. When applied under the liquid metal it acts as a primer coat.

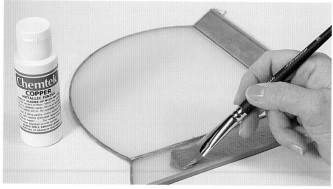

2 APPLY THE COPPER LAYER
With the no. 14 flat shader, brush on one coat of the Copper Metallic Finish. Let this dry. Since the Copper is applied to glass you'll need two to three coats. Let this dry.

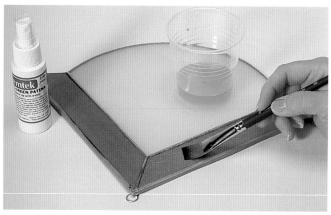

3 APPLY THE PATINA
Apply one more coat of Copper and allow it to dry until tacky. Brush on one medium coat of Green Patina. Allow to dry naturally. It will begin to oxidize in about five minutes.

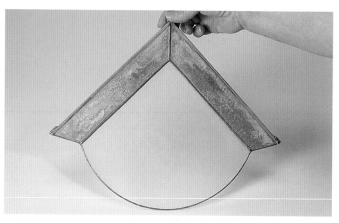

4 THE RESULTS
When the edges are dry, decide if you like the results. If you want more patina, apply another layer of Green patina. If you are satisfied, apply two coats of the Aqueous Sealer.

5 CORRECTING FOR TOO MUCH PATINA
Apply another layer of Copper over the patina and allow it to oxidize from underneath the metal. Let dry. Finish as in step 4.

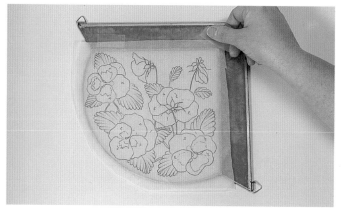

6 ATTACH THE PATTERN
Tape the design, right side to the back of the prepared glass, beginning at the corner.

PAINT THE LEAVES

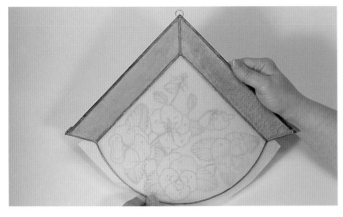

1 VIEWING THE PATTERN
The design is easily seen through the etched glass. There is no need to apply the pattern directly to the glass.

2 THE DARK SIDE OF THE LEAVES
Load Margot's Multi-load brush fully in Gamal Green and pull through Antique Gold Deep. Face the light side of the brush to the top or right of the design. Begin the dark side with a stroke next to the center vein and work down to the bottom of leaf.

> **HINT**
> I like to paint all the dark sides while I have this load in the brush.

3 THE LIGHT SIDE OF THE LEAVES
Reload as for the dark side, but pull through a little Raw Linen on the Antique Gold Deep side of the brush. Again face the light side to the top or right of the design, begin painting with the center vein and work down. Repeat for all the leaves.

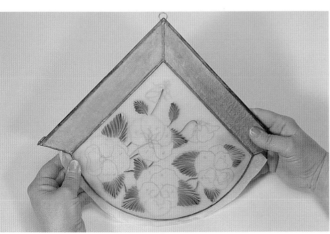

4 COMPLETE THE STEMS AND LEAVES
With the same triple load pull in all the stems using the same technique as in previous steps.

PAINT THE PANSIES

1 BACK PETAL ON PANSIES
Tuck the pansy petals in around the painted leaves, not over the leaves. If a painted leaf ended up in the pansy petal space, just dribble the edge of the petal around the leaf.

Load fully in Dioxazine Purple, pull through Raw Sienna and pick up Magnolia White. Face the White side of the brush toward the outer edge of the petal. Dribble, catch and pull to the calyx (center of the flower) staying within the pattern.

2 SECOND BACK PETAL
Begin the dribble at the outer edge of the petal. Continue the dribble across the completed petal. Catch the dribble where you ended it and pull to the calyx, changing direction as you work back across the dribble. Stop at the dotted line indicated on the pattern. This will allow space for the yellow throat to show. Wash the brush.

3 THROAT
Thin Yellow Light about fifty-fifty with water. Pat thinned color onto the throat area and fade up into the painted back petals. Tap an uneven edge on the front. Wash the brush.

> **HINT**
> Refer to the pattern for the placement of the faces but freehand them in. Look at lots of different pansies and you will see a vast variety of faces. Just keep them a bit ragged.

4 FRONT SIDE PETALS

Both petals are painted the same way. Load fully in Cranberry Wine, pull through Raw Sienna and pick up Magnolia White. Begin the dribble where the side petal is under the front petal, stopping when you get to the yellow throat. Begin catching the dribble and pull it to the calyx.

5 FRONT PETAL

Refresh the brush load by tapping the dark side perfectly flat with Cranberry Wine and picking up Magnolia White on the light side of the brush. This petal is done in two sections so that the white doesn't have a chance to dry before you can get back to catch it. Begin the dribble at the middle of the petal. Pull to the calyx and stop each stroke when you reach the throat. Repeat for the other half of the petal. Wash the brush.

6 PANSY FACE

Flatten the brush on both sides with Dioxazine Purple. Using the chisel edge of the brush, "touch, lift and cut" on the side front petal, always lifting to the calyx. Keep the brush flattened by pressing against the palette when reloading. On the front petal, bring the strokes up into the yellow throat. The strokes are uneven.

HINT

Raw Sienna is used between the Dioxazine Purple and the Cranberry Wine to reduce the intensity.

PAINT THE PANSIES, CONTINUED

7 ADDING THE DETAILS
With Dioxazine Purple in the brush, pull in one "touch, lift and cut" stroke for the very center of each front petal. Wash the brush. Be sure to turn your work to make painting more comfortable.

8 ADDING TURNBACKS TO PETALS
Load the brush in Magnolia White and pick up a little Magnolia White. Face the picked-up White to the outside of the pansy. Touch down, connecting the top white edge of the side petals with the top edge of the middle petal. Repeat for the other side.

THE COMPLETED TURNBACK
Evaluate the finished flower. Look for any areas that need help or a bit of interest.

9 PAINT THE TURNBACKS ON THE OUTSIDE EDGES
Load the brush in Magnolia White and pick up more Magnolia White. With the white facing the interior of the petal, begin the stroke on one white edge, gently press the tip of the bristles sending the white inward. Release slowly and connect back to the white edge and lift off. Do not apply too many turnbacks or it will overwhelm the flower.

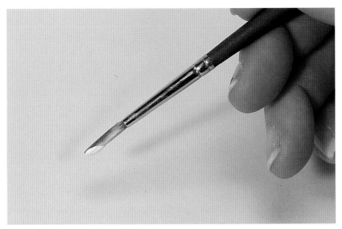

10 FOUR COLOR BRUSH LOAD
Load fully in Yellow Light. Pull through Antique Gold Deep on one side. Turn the brush over and pull through Cranberry Wine (just a smear). Turn the brush back over and pick up Magnolia White on the Yellow Light side.

11 MIDDLE OPEN PANSY
Complete this pansy in the same manner as the other two using the Cranberry Wine load for the back petals. For the front petal use the four color yellow load, but apply it in the same manner as you did for the previous pansies (see pages 64-66). Wash the brush.

HINT
To reload, gently wipe off the white and on the light side pull through Antique Gold Deep. Pull through Yellow Light, turn the brush over and tap into the Cranberry Wine with the flat of the dark side. Turn the brush back over and pick up white on the light side.

FRONT VIEW PANSIES COMPLETED

BACK FACING PANSY COMPLETED

12 BACK FACING PANSY—FIRST TWO PETALS
Reload in Cranberry Wine, and pull through white. Begin with the petal furthest back. For the second petals pick up white.

PAINT THE PANSY BUDS

1 SIDE VIEW PANSY BUD—YELLOW PETALS
Load the brush as you did for the yellow pansy, but not much Cranberry Wine on brush. Dribble, catch and pull to the calyx to form the bud. Wash the brush.

2 LAST PETAL ON SIDE-VIEW BUD
Load the brush with the Cranberry Wine combination. This time start at the outer edge, dribble across the middle petal. Push the bristles slightly to the right so the petal flares out. Catch the dribble, lift and cut to the calyx. The last stroke forms the outer edge of the petal.

3 THE CLOSED BUD
Load the brush with the Dioxazine Purple combination. Dribble, catch and pull. All the dribbles begin at the top of the petal. Wash the brush.

4 FINISHING TOUCHES
Buff the dried acrylic paint with a soft, white cloth until you have a satin finish. The sealers in the acrylic paint are being polished. No further sealing is necessary. Hang and enjoy!

THE COMPLETED PANSIES ON GLASS

MORNING GLORIES GARDEN JOURNAL

I enjoy spending time in my garden. Seeing the morning glories winding their way around a trellis or hanging over a fence in masses of blooms is a magnificent sight. It almost takes your breath away. My favorites are the traditional blues with a few pink ones peeking out here and there. You can make morning glories whatever color you want just by changing the picked-up color on your brush.

Morning glories are so beautiful, a word most gardeners would like to use to describe their own gardens. What better choice for the cover of this garden journal.

The brass edging gives the journal an aged look as if it has been out in the garden often. I take photos of my garden each year to keep track of the progress and changes that occur.

If you are not interested in gardening, you can leave the words off and use the wooden journal for a wedding or baby shower, or apply the design to a stool or small side table. How about trailing morning glories around a window frame? Once you master the few strokes needed to paint these morning glories, you will be able to paint them anywhere you choose.

Do not transfer the tendrils. They are better painted freehand.

Garden Journal

Margot © 1999

(above) This pattern may be hand-traced or photocopied for personal use only. Enlarge at 160.5% to bring it up to full size.

(left) This tracing shows the sequence of painting the petals and buds.

PREPARE THE SURFACE

1 Sand the wood and seal it with wood sealer. Let this dry and sand it again with the crumpled brown paper bag.

2 Using the 1-inch (25mm) flat wash/glaze brush, basecoat the front and back sections, inside and out in Eggshell.

3 Apply Aqueous Sealer to the edge pieces, front and back, as a primer.

4 Apply one coat of Brass Metallic Finish to the edge piece. Let dry.

5 Apply a second coat of Brass and while wet, spritz on Aqua Blue Patina with the heaviest application near the post holes. Allow to dry.

6 Sponge on Brass over any areas that are too heavily patinaed. The Brass will oxidize from underneath but won't be quite as bold. Allow the patina to get on the metal hinges and posts, so they can age also.

7 Allow to dry and apply one coat of Aqueous Sealer to all patinaed surfaces to protect the finish.

8 Trace everything from the pattern onto tracing paper. Use the dotted lines to indicate the shadow leaves. Transfer everything but the tendrils.

MATERIALS

PAINT: (D) = DELTA CERAMCOAT ACRYLICS; (DA) = DECOART AMERICANA

Magnolia White (D)

Yellow Light (DA)

Eggshell (DA)

Gamal Green (D)

French Grey Blue (DA)

Wild Rose (D)

SURFACE
- Wooden album available at most craft stores and from mail-order catalogs

BRUSHES
- Margot's Multi-load
- $\frac{1}{2}$-inch (12mm) angle shader
- 1-inch (25mm) flat wash/glaze

CHEMTEK PRODUCTS
- Aqueous Sealer
- Brass Metallic Finish
- Aqua Blue Patina

ADDITIONAL SUPPLIES
- Sandpaper
- Sea sponge
- Crumpled brown paper bag
- Tracing paper
- Gray graphite paper
- Stylus
- J.W. Etc. First Step Wood Sealer

Paint the Morning Glories

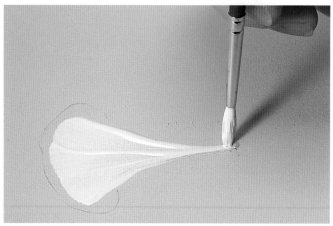

1 Pulling in the White Base Strokes

Load Margot's Multi-load brush with enough white to lay down the base strokes, because the flower color is pulled into the wet white. Keep the side of the throat narrow since that is where it tucks into the calyx. Don't let the strokes cross over each other. Lay them down next to one another.

2 The Blue Dribble

Leave the white in the brush and pick up French Grey Blue on one side of the brush. Face the blue to the petal's outer edge, and begin the dribble slightly before the base strokes. Set the brush down under the dribble. Press the bristles open, catch the dribble and pull it to the calyx.

3 The Side-View Morning Glory

Immediately begin the lift, turn and cut stroke keeping the blue along the left edge of base and allowing the blue to fade out into the white trumpet area by releasing pressure on the bristles. Pick up more blue, set the brush down under the dribble in the middle of the flower, blue side up. Gently press the bristles open, but not touching the edge of the first blue

stroke. Complete this stroke allowing a white space to remain between the blue strokes. This creates the petal veins. Reload in blue and complete the third stroke. Keep the blue along the right edge of the trumpet as you pull the stroke. This is a completed side view and can be used as is or you can go on to the next step.

Hint

Morning glories are a good example of controlled freedom discussed on page 16. The "controlled" part is that you have only three strokes to get the correct look and they need to be precise. The "freedom" is that you can change the design easily. If you paint a great side view, it can stay as a side view. If it is just okay or has a problem, you can turn it into a front view by adding the turned front petal. Do not hesitate to make design changes to make the technique work for you.

4 THE FRONT-VIEW MORNING GLORY

Turn the flower sideways. Dribble French Grey Blue down and across the side view, connecting with the existing blue at each side. Face the blue toward the trumpet base. With the knife edge of the brush, cut in a smile line. This will determine the width of the turned-back petal edge.

5 THE TURNED EDGE PETALS

Turn the flower upside down and begin to catch the dribble in the middle of the turned front petal, stopping at the smile line. Pull in from the outer edge, turning the flower as you paint. Keep pulling in until new stokes match the lines in the previously painted back strokes. Quickly repeat on the other side, working from the middle of the turned petal.

6 THE FULL FRONT VIEW, COMPLETED FRONT AND SIDE VIEWS

For the large flower be sure to lay down a good amount of white. This flower is painted the same as the previous side views, except it takes more strokes to complete. Also, the front turnback is deeper. Pick up French Grey Blue and then pick up Wild Rose. If you prefer, pick up Wild Rose first and then pick up French Grey Blue and the result will be a pink flower streaked with blue.

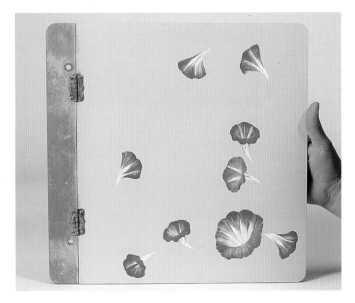

ADD THE BUDS, VINES AND LEAVES

1 COMPLETED BUDS
Look at the bud diagram at the bottom of page 72. Load the brush in Magnolia White. Turn the bud upside down and base the whole bud in one "press, lift and cut stroke." Reload in white and pull through a *tiny bit* of French Grey Blue. Begin at the top of the bud. Turn the blue side of the brush toward the top of the stroke. Pull in each section in an "S" shape. Start on the chisel edge, add pressure, pull across and end on the chisel edge. Wash the brush.

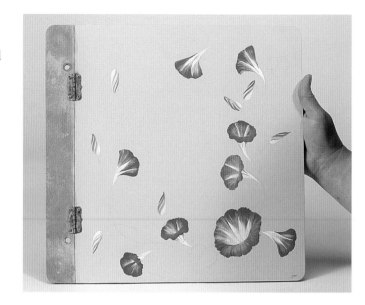

2 COMPLETED VINES
Flatten both sides of the brush in Gamal Green. Use the chisel edge, hold the handle straight up and pull in all the vines, leaf stems and bud stems. Allow the brush to slightly rotate in your fingers to keep it on the chisel edge.

3 PAINTING THE LEAVES
Begin the leaf stroke with the multi- load brush. Line up the flat edge of the brush with the back edge of the leaf. Fan out the bristles on the right side by exerting pressure on the handle. The left-side bristles don't move. Begin to lift and cut on the knife edge to create tip of the leaf. Repeat for the left side.

If there is a hole in the middle of your leaf, pull in a third stroke to fill the space starting at the base and lifting to the tip. To prevent that from happening next time, make sure the brush handle stays in place and that only the bristles fan out forming the leaf.

FINISHING TOUCHES

CALYXES, SEPALS AND TENDRILS
Paint the calyxes, sepals and tendrils with Margot's Multi-load brush loaded with Gamal Green and Magnolia White.

SHADOW LEAVES
Make a thin wash of Gamal Green, approximately 20 percent color to 80 percent water. Make the wash on the palette. Load the multi-load brush in thinned color, touch off the tip to a paper towel to remove excess color, and pull in the shadow leaves indicated by the dotted lines on the pattern. Paint three or four leaves with each brush load so you end up with varying values of leaves. Wash the brush.

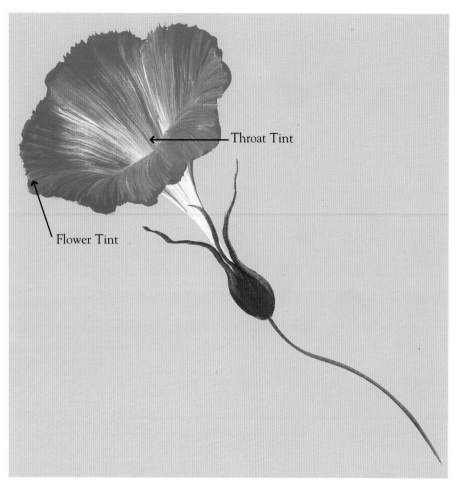

Throat Tint

Flower Tint

TINTS IN FLOWER THROATS

Make a very light wash of Yellow Light (10 percent color to 90 percent water). Do not substitute Light Yellow or any other pale yellow for Yellow Light, because those colors have white added and your wash will be cloudy. Load the brush and touch the tip to a paper towel. Place the yellow in the throats of each front-view flower.

FLOWER TINTS

Using the angle shader or the multi-load brush, place tints of Wild Rose on the blue flowers and a hint of French Grey Blue on the pink flowers. Wash the brush.

Shade the buds using the angle shader with a side load of thinned Gamal Green. Pull the long edge of the brush through the thinned color. Stroke once on the wet palette to be sure the color is very thin and is on one-half of the bristles. Face the color toward the bottom of the bud. Start on the chisel edge. Pull across the bud in a "U" or "C" shape and end up back on the chisel edge.

HINT

You can always go back and add another wash of color if it is too light, but it is very hard to work around tints that are too dark. As you place the tint be ready with a damp paper towel. If the color looks too strong, lift it off immediately.

LETTERING

Letters are formed with the multi-load brush using "press, lift and cut" strokes in Gamal Green. Paint the tendrils using the no. 1 script liner rolled to a point in Gamal Green thinned to the consistency of ink. Keep the handle up and stay on the very tip of the brush.

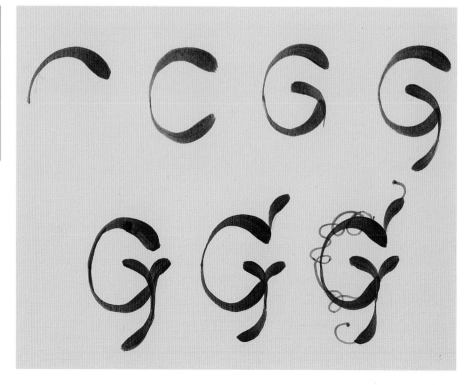

EDGING

Using the 3/4-inch shader, dampen the outer edge of the cover with clear water. While the edge is damp, float thinned Gamal Green with a 1/2-inch angle shader along the outer edge using a pat-and-pull motion. Don't try to paint the whole edge in one long stroke, which is hard to do and does not look natural. Do one edge at a time keeping the surface dampened with the clear water for a soft look.

VARNISH AND WAX

Allow to dry twenty-four hours. Apply two to three coats of varnish over painted and patinaed metal surfaces. Finish with a coat of finishing wax.

PROJECT

ANGEL-WING ROSES TABLE

This little table painted with roses and liquid metals is eye-catching because of the contrasts, light against dark, bright against subtle. The design is easy to adapt to different surfaces, a matching tray, perhaps, or a box. The red/green complementary color scheme is also pleasing to the eye.

I call this rose an Angel-wing Rose because the side petals of the skirt look like angel's wings reaching up to the sky. This rose will be the foundation for the more advanced roses we'll see in Project 6. The border leaf trim is an adaptation of the pansy leaf in Project 3 (see page 63).

MATERIALS

PAINT: DELTA CERAMCOAT ACRYLICS

Opaque Red

Walnut

Gamal Green

Materials List continued on page 84

Trim for bottom and top shelves of table. Adjust to fit by lengthening or shortening the stem and leaves.

Design for bottom shelf

Tabletop design. Do not transfer small details. Transfer the leaves as shown. Do not outline.

Center of design

These patterns may be hand-traced or photocopied for personal use only. Enlarge at 167% to bring them up to full size.

Prepare the Surface

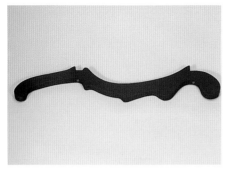

1 Basecoat the Table and Legs
Sand the shelves and legs. Seal the wood with wood sealer, let dry and sand again with a brown paper bag. Smoothly basecoat all surfaces with Gamal Green.

2 Applying the Aqueous Sealer
Brush on one coat of Aqueous Sealer to each side of the table legs. Place Gold, Copper, Brass and Dark Bronze Metallic Finishes on a foam plate.

3 Sponge on the Metallic Finishes
Dampen a silk sponge, and pick up two different metals each time. Don't make a pattern with the sponge, turn it as you pounce. Don't stay in one place too long.

4 Apply the Patina
Randomly spritz Aqua Blue Patina over the wet metals on one side of each leg and allow to dry naturally. Repeat for the rest of the sides on all the legs.

5 Fully Developed Patina
This is the look of fully developed patina when dry. This is a fairly heavy application. If you like this, you can skip the next step and go straight to the Insta-Neutralizer. I prefer a softer look, which you can get with step 6.

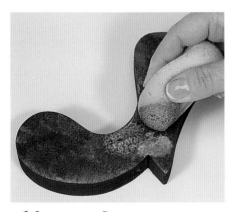

6 Soften the Patina
Randomly sponge a thin layer of the same metals over the patinaed areas. This new layer will oxidize from underneath and give a more subtle look. Allow this to dry naturally.

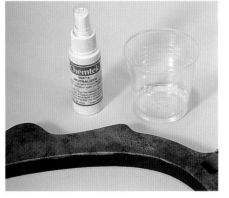

7 Apply the Insta-Neutralizer
To prevent any further oxidation from taking place, brush on one thin coat of Insta-Neutralizer. Allow to dry and brush on a coat of Aqueous Sealer to protect the finish. Touch up the edges of the legs with Gamal Green.

Hint
Use caution when applying the patina. The patina goes on like water and within five minutes the oxidation will begin. The keyword here is "begin." Oxidation occurs on wet metal as long as it is wet. The sponged metals will continue to oxidize as they dry. Resist the temptation to apply more patina until you see the finished results. Oxidation is complete when the patina looks dull and powdery.

PAINT THE ROSES

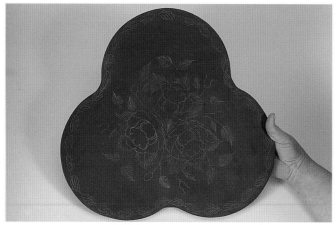

1 TRANSFER DESIGN
Lightly transfer the design to the surface using white graphite paper and the stylus. Transfer all lines for the leaves. If caught under the paint, the individual lines look like veins. If you outline the leaves, the graphite is caught under the paint at the tip and looks like dash marks.

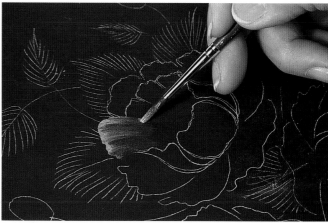

2 FIRST STROKE ON THE ROSE
Place Opaque Red, Walnut and Gold Metallic Finish on the palette. Load Margot's Multi-load brush fully in the red mix (Opaque Red + Walnut), pick up Gold. Dribble across the first petal. Remove the excess Gold on a damp paper towel. Face the Gold side up, catch and pull toward the calyx. Use this same load for all the roses in this project.

3 BACK PETALS COMPLETE
Repeat the previous steps for the other petals in the back. Reload for each petal.

4 SECOND ROW COMPLETE
Refer to the pattern on page 82 for placement. Do not try to be exact or line them up with the back row. Remember to pull to the calyx.

MATERIALS CONTINUED

SURFACE
- Jacobean Table from Sechtem's Wood Products

BRUSHES
- Margot's Multi-load
- 1-inch (25mm) flat wash/glaze
- no. 1 liner

CHEMTEK PRODUCTS
- Aqueous Sealer
- Metallic Finishes
  Gold
  Copper
  Brass
  Dark Bronze
- Aqua Blue Patina
- Insta-Neutralizer

ADDITIONAL SUPPLIES
- Silk sponge
- Tracing paper
- White graphite paper
- Stylus
- Sandpaper
- J.W. Etc. First Step Wood Sealer
- Crumpled brown paper bag

5 THE MIDDLE PETALS

Dribble Gold along the top of the petal keeping the sides higher than the middle. This will help to ensure a rounded inner bowl. Turn the Gold side to the right and push out to form the side of the petal. Reload, turning the Gold side to the left and repeat. Turn the Gold side up and pull in a straight stroke in the middle of the petal. Pull in the curved strokes on both sides to fill in the petal.

6 THE SIDE INNER PETALS

Dribble Gold across the top of the petal just barely connecting with the back edges (keep the bowl rounded). Cut in right next to the middle petal. Pull the stroke in right next to, but not touching, the middle petal and follow the curve of the bowl. Pull each stroke toward the calyx, following the curve of the petal. I like to refer to this stroke as "in at the waist and out at the hips." Both side petals are painted this same way.

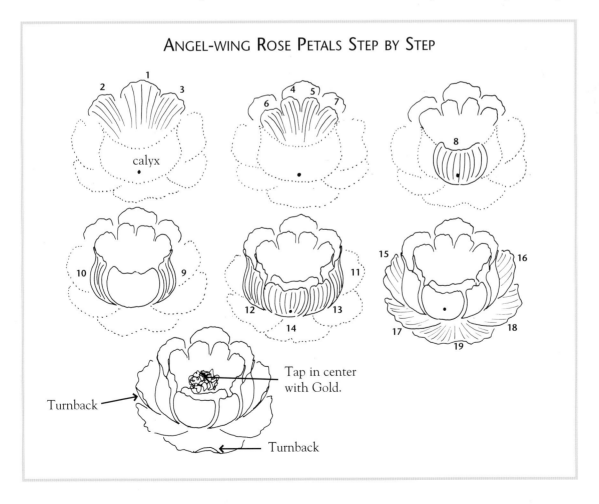

ANGEL-WING ROSE PETALS STEP BY STEP

PAINT THE ROSES, CONTINUED

7 THE SIDES OF THE OUTER BOWL
Catch the edge of the back outer row. Dribble partway across the side petal, staying under the edge of the bowl front. Pull strokes to fill the petal, following the established curves. Do the same for each side.

8 THE THIRD PETAL IN OUTER BOWL
Dribble over both the right inner side petal and about a third of the way onto the inner middle petal. Pull the strokes from the right.

9 THE FOURTH PETAL IN OUTER BOWL
Dribble across the top of the last petal, over the left inner petal and over the inner middle petal. Push out both sides, next to but not touching the outer petals that you just painted. Pull the strokes to fill in the petal, curving the strokes to follow the curves.

10 THE BACK PETALS ON THE SKIRT—THE ANGEL WINGS
Begin the dribble at the top of the petal. Push the Gold out as you cut in toward the calyx. Catch and pull the strokes in, but do not touch the bowl. This creates a shadowed effect and keeps you off the painted bowl.

11 THE NEXT LAYER OF SKIRT PETALS

Paint these exactly as the previous row, but be careful to leave a little space between the previous petals.

12 THE MIDDLE SKIRT PETAL

Turn the rose upside down. Dribble across the outer edge of the petal. Begin to pull in strokes at one side following the curve of the previous petal. Begin to straighten out as you work towards the middle of the petal and then start to follow the curve of the previous petal on the other side.

13 THE TURNBACKS ON THE SKIRT PETALS

Flatten the brush by loading it in the red mix. Pick up a little Gold. Face the Gold side of the brush toward the inside of the petal. Begin at outer edge and connect with the back edge of the petal. Then push Gold towards the petal, release the pressure and cut to the calyx. When painting turnbacks there are a few things to keep in mind: (1) Just because I paint a turnback doesn't mean that *your* petal will need one. (2) Paint the turnbacks after completing the whole flower. Does an edge look really ragged? Is the edge too flat or boring? Does an area lack interest? These are the points to consider. If I show a turnback in the photo but your petal looks great— leave it alone! Use turnbacks sparingly. Too many turnbacks and your elegant flower will look cluttered.

14 THE CENTER OF THE ROSE

Roll the brush to a point in Gold. Dip the tip into a little Gold and tap in the center allowing some of the background to show through. Repeat these steps for the other two roses, varying the placement.

HINT
Turn the flower as you're painting to allow the dribble to be painted in the most comfortable position for your hand.

PAINT THE ROSEBUDS

1 THE BACK PETALS OF THE OPEN ROSEBUD
For the rosebuds, do not pick up as much Gold as you would for the roses. Dribble higher in the middle of the petal.

Be sure to remove excess Gold before catching. Pull the two petals of the back row to the calyx.

2 CENTER BACK PETAL SECOND ROW
Dribble across the middle with the first petal higher. This helps retain the illusion of roundness. Catch and pull to the calyx.

3 CLOSING THE CENTER
Dribble about halfway across the back petals in a downward facing arc. Connect with the opposite edge and dribble across for the other side of the petal. Again, just barely catch the dribble with the bristles and pull towards the calyx.

4 THE SIDE PETALS ON THE OPEN ROSEBUD
Dribble a little more than halfway across the bud staying under the center. Flare the brush out a bit then lift to the

calyx. Catch and pull the dribble, straightening the stroke and ending up with an in-at-the-waist-and-out-at-the-hip stroke.

Turnbacks

5 SIDE PETAL OF SKIRT
Dribble, catch and pull the strokes without touching the rosebud. The strokes are directed toward the calyx. These petals look as if they were coming out from behind the bud.

6 ADD THE FRONT TURNBACKS
Turn the bud upside down. Reload in Red and pick up Gold. Barely connect with the bottom edge of the skirt. Push the Gold away from the bud as you come across the front. Lift to the tip of the brush and cut to the calyx. Wipe off the excess Gold. Pull the dribble blending with the existing side petal. Do not let these strokes extend into the bowl.

7 BACK OF CLOSED BUD
Dribble, catch and pull, exerting pressure on the side strokes to form an oval.

8 SIDE PETALS CLOSED BUD
Connect with back edge. Dribble, catch and pull allowing second petal to cross over the first petal.

COMPLETED ROSES, OPEN BUDS AND CLOSED BUDS

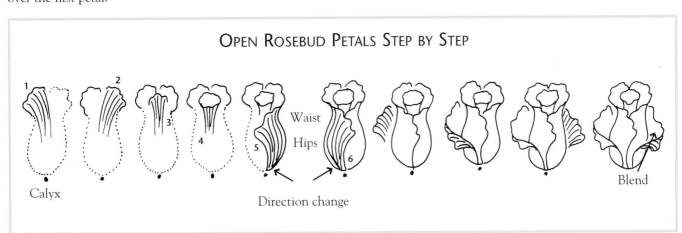

OPEN ROSEBUD PETALS STEP BY STEP

Calyx Waist Hips Direction change Blend

PAINT THE LEAVES, STEMS AND CALYXES

1 PULL THE STEMS AND LEAVES
Load the multi-load brush with Gamal Green and pull through Gold. Face the Gold toward the outer edge of the tabletop. Pull in the stems that are furthest back in the design by adding pressure under the bud to form the calyx. Then turn, lift and cut to complete the stem. Pull in leaf stems. Then fill in the leaves with touch, lift and cut strokes. Cut the stroke in toward the center vein. Do not touch the roses with any of the strokes. On the top side of the leaf the strokes will fall in the same direction. On the underside they may change direction. Remember to paint the first two strokes at the tip and follow the curve of the center vein line and keep them short. Gradually change direction on the underside of the leaf and retain the graceful curve.

2 ALL LEAVES AND STEMS BEHIND ROSES COMPLETE

3 THE FILLER LEAVES AND STEMS
Pull in the remaining leaves and stems. Your brush should not become too gold. Reload Gamal Green as necessary to keep the leaves green.

4 ALL LEAVES COMPLETE

5 SEPALS ON OPEN ROSEBUDS

Use a fresh load of Gamal Green pulled through Gold. Face the gold side of the brush up. Pull in the two back sepals. Position the brush at the calyx with the chisel edge parallel with the bottom of the bud. Slide on the chisel, press open the bristles and immediately turn, lift and cut. On the open bud the sepals fall away. Look closely at the photo and note that the sepal is not straight. Let it gently curve.

For the middle sepal, pull through more Gold, so it is lighter than the back sepals. The sepals cover part of the closed bud and wrap around the sides. Use the "press, lift and cut stroke" with a very small stroke.

6 FINISHING TOUCHES TO THE FLORAL DESIGN

Add tiny comma strokes (remember they are "press, lift and cut" strokes) and a few solid filler leaves using one or two strokes to form the solid leaves with Gold directed to the outer edge of the leaf. Refer to pages 18-19 for detailed instruction on filler leaves. If any petals need to be separated, use thinned Gamal Green and the $\frac{1}{2}$-inch (12mm) angle shader.

LEAVES STEP BY STEP

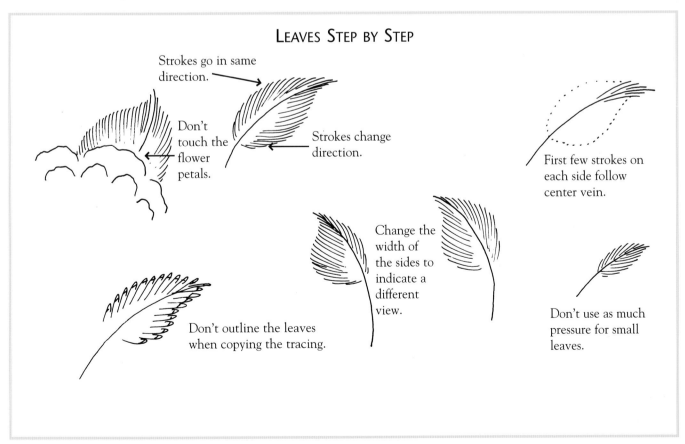

Strokes go in same direction.

Don't touch the flower petals.

Strokes change direction.

First few strokes on each side follow center vein.

Change the width of the sides to indicate a different view.

Don't outline the leaves when copying the tracing.

Don't use as much pressure for small leaves.

THE FINISHING TOUCHES

1 METALLIC LEAF BORDER
Wash the multi-load brush. Place Gold and Copper on a dry palette. Load the brush in Gold. Then pull one side through Copper. Face the Gold side to the outer edge and pull in the center vein and stem. Pull the strokes to complete the leaves. These are the same strokes used for the Pansy leaves in Project 3, page 63. Wipe the brush and reload as necessary to keep the Gold and Copper separate.

2 DESIGN ON BOTTOM SHELF
The design on the bottom shelf is painted the same way as the leaf border. The curved lines are painted with the no. 1 script liner loaded with slightly thinned Gold.

3 APPLY THE WASH TO SHELF EDGES

Thin Gold with water (1:1) and apply as a wash to the edge of the shelves using the 1-inch (25mm) flat wash/glaze brush. Repeat if necessary. Let dry twenty-four hours and varnish. Let the varnish cure for twenty-four hours and then wax all the surfaces.

THE COMPLETED TABLE

PROJECT 6

A GARDEN OF ROSES SEWING BOX

This rose doesn't really have a name, but it reminds me of a hybrid tea rose. It begins with the opening rosebud we saw in Project 5. The brush load is different, but the strokes remain the same. Additional layers of petals are added to show the rose at different stages of opening.

In this project you will continue to build on the skills you've learned in previous projects. Tints, washes and glazing techniques are being added to that growing list of skills.

The finishing techniques taught on this box can be used on any surface. It has a faux tortoiseshell finish, faux burled walnut finish and eggshell crackle over a painted area. The pattern and techniques can be used on furniture, frames and household items, just to name a few. Be sure to adapt these designs to your own personal taste.

PAINT: (D) = DELTA CERAMCOAT ACRYLICS; (DA) = DECOART AMERICANA ACRYLICS

Magnolia
White (D)

Raw Linen
(D)

Eggshell
(DA)

Antique Gold
Deep (DA)

Raw Sienna (D)

Burnt Sienna
(D)

Opaque Red
(D)

Gamal Green
(D)

Dark Forest
Green (D)

Walnut
(D)

Black
(D)

Materials List continued on page 97.

FRONT AND BACK PANELS

END PANEL

TOP OF BOX

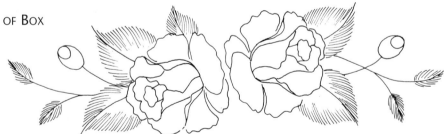

These patterns may
be hand-traced or
photocopied for
personal use only.
Enlarge at 189% to
bring them up to
full size.

INSIDE LID

PREPARE THE SURFACE

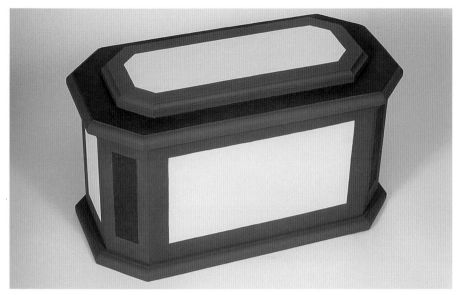

1 BASECOAT THE BOX
Sand and seal the box and sand again with the crumpled brown paper bag. To basecoat the following areas you will measure and mark measurements with a pencil. (See measurements for the panels below left.) You can then tape off the sections or, if you have a steady hand, just pull the no. 14 flat shader along the edge of the pencil line. All the light areas on the box are painted with Raw Linen.

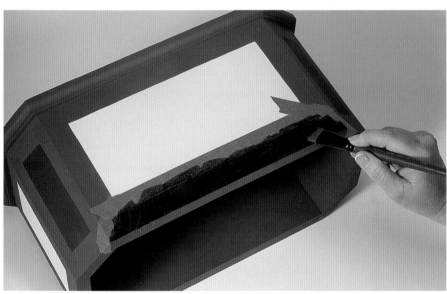

2 APPLY THINNED DARK BRONZE
Tape off a section protecting the Raw Linen panel, creating mitered corners with the tape to create the illusion of wood veneer. Thin Dark Bronze Metallic 4:1 with waterand apply with a no. 14 flat brush to the taped off sections.

MEASUREMENTS FOR THE PANELS

Panel on top of the lid: Measure in ¾-inch (1.9cm) from each edge. Basecoat with Raw Linen.

Panel under the lid: 2 inches (5cm) in from all the edges. Basecoat with Raw Linen.

Panels on the ends of the box bottom: ¾-inch (1.9cm) in from the sides and 1-inch (2.5cm) from the top and bottom edges. Basecoat with Raw Linen.

Front and back side panels: 1 inch (2.5cm) in from each edge. Basecoat with Raw Linen.

Flat outer area on top of the lid: Basecoat with Dark Forest Green.

Panels on the slanted sides of box bottom: 1 inch (2.5cm) from top and bottom edges and ½-inch (1.2cm) in from the sides. Basecoat with Dark Forest Green.

All other areas inside and out of the top and bottom of the box: Basecoat with Burnt Sienna.

MATERIALS CONT.

SURFACE
- Antique Sewing Box available from Valhalla Designs

CHEMTEK PRODUCTS
- Metallic Finishes
  Gold   Copper
  Brass   Dark Bronze

BRUSHES
- Margot's Multi-load
- 1-inch (25mm) wash/glaze
- no. 14 flat shader
- ½-inch (12mm) angle shader

ADDITIONAL SUPPLIES
- Delta Ceramcoat Two Step Fine Crackle
- Gray graphite paper
- Low tack tape
- Plastic wrap
- Rubbing alcohol
- Spritzer bottle

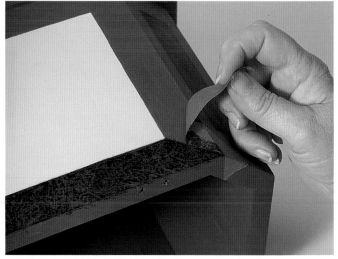

3 CREATE THE FAUX BURLED WALNUT

Place Dark Bronze Metallic Finish on a foam plate and thin slightly with water about four parts Dark Bronze to one part water. Apply it to the surface with the 1-inch (25mm) flat wash/glaze brush. Immediately pounce wadded plastic wrap into the wet Dark Bronze to lift off excess and create faux burled walnut. Turn the wad of plastic in a different direction each time you pounce to avoid a repetitive pattern.

4 REMOVE TAPE

Remove the tape while the finish is wet by pulling straight up on the tape. Complete all the Burnt Sienna areas on bottom side of the lid, the sides and top edge of the box bottom using these instructions. Save the section on top of the lid for after the tortoiseshell technique is varnished.

> **HINT**
> Work on one side at a time. Apply the technique to the top and bottom sections and allow to dry. Then go on to the side sections.

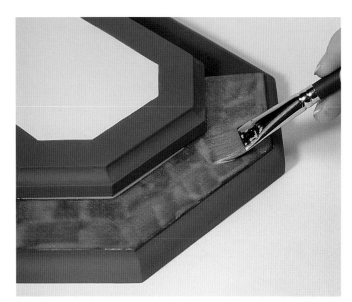

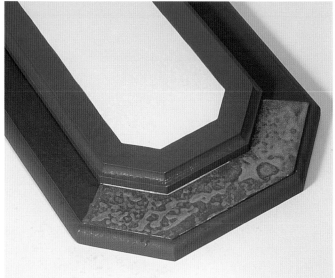

5 FAUX TORTOISESHELL TECHNIQUE—BRASS LAYER

Test steps 5 and 6 on a scrap of wood to be sure the Brass will disperse. If it does not, add more water. Thin Brass Metallic two parts Brass to one part water. Apply Brass to the box lid one section at a time with the no. 14 flat brush.

6 SPRITZ WITH ALCOHOL

Immediately spritz alcohol to cause the brass to disperse. Repeat to complete the remaining green areas one section at a time. Let this dry and apply one coat of gloss varnish.

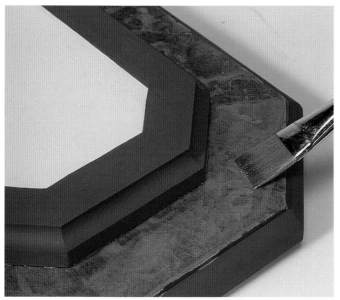

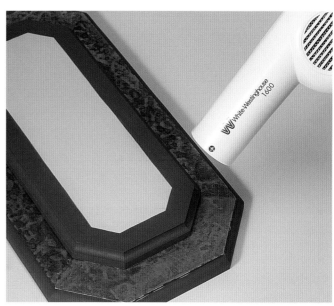

7 Faux Tortoiseshell Technique—Copper Layer

Thin Copper Metallic with water (2:1) and apply with a no. 14 flat brush. Spritz with alcohol working the lid in four sections. Let this dry and apply one coat of gloss varnish. The four small panels on the box bottom are worked differently. Apply a thin layer of Copper with the no. 14 flat brush, wipe the brush and load with a little Brass, brush on a few patches of Brass, wipe the brush and blend the edges of the Brass into the Copper. Let this dry and apply one coat of satin varnish.

8 Speed-up the Drying Time

The drying time can be reduced by using a hair dryer. Stay far enough away from the surface so the forced air does not disturb the metal.

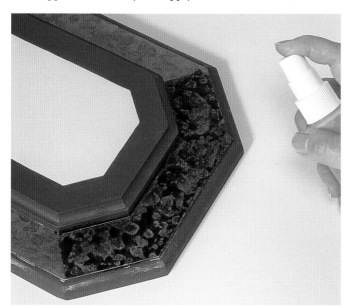

9 Dark Bronze Layer

Thin Dark Bronze Metallic with water (2:1) and spritz with alcohol, working in one section at a time. This step is also applied to the four small panels on the box bottom. Prop the box bottom so the panels are level when applying the Dark Bronze/alcohol technique to prevent runs.

10 Backgrounds Complete

Brush one coat of gloss varnish on the tortoiseshell areas and let dry. Apply the Dark Bronze/plastic wrap technique in Step 3 on the Burnt Sienna areas. Wash the brush. Thin Gold just a little and brush on all routed edges. The Burnt Sienna should be visible through the Gold.

PAINT THE ROSEBUDS

1 CLOSED AND OPEN ROSEBUDS
Apply the patterns to all Raw Linen insets. Load the Multi-load brush in the red mix (Opaque Red + Walnut), pull through Raw Sienna and pick up Magnolia White. Paint the closed buds and bowls of open rosebuds, directing white in the same directions as the instructions in Project 5 (see pages 86-87). The open rosebud at this stage is the basis for all the roses in this design. Side and skirt petals are added to show different stages of a rose opening.

2 ADDING THE SKIRTS TO OPEN BUDS
Pull the skirts on the open buds. Add the full petals on both sides as shown here or paint only partial skirts as described in Project 5 (see pages 86-87).

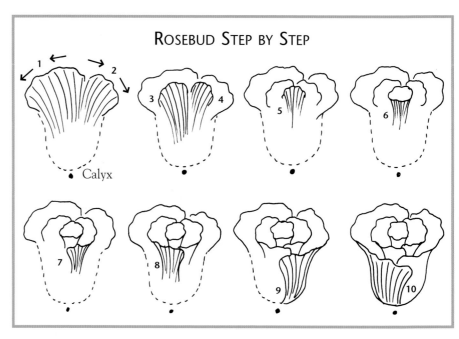

ROSEBUD STEP BY STEP

THE END PANEL OPENING ROSES

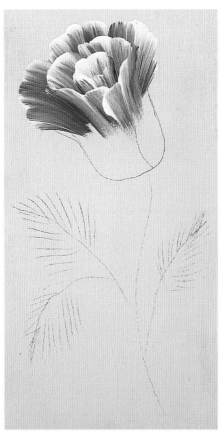

1 OPENING ROSE ON THE END PANELS
This version adds another layer to the basic bud. Start with the three petals on the back row, paint two more and then the back half of the middle petal. Remember to pull towards the calyx, white side up.

2 CONNECT THE TWO INNER LAYERS
Connect the middle with each side and pull in overlapping petals, keeping the center oval. Since there are two more layers to paint, these petals get pulled towards the calyx. See "Add the Next Two Layers," Step 3 on page 102.

OPEN ROSE END PANELS

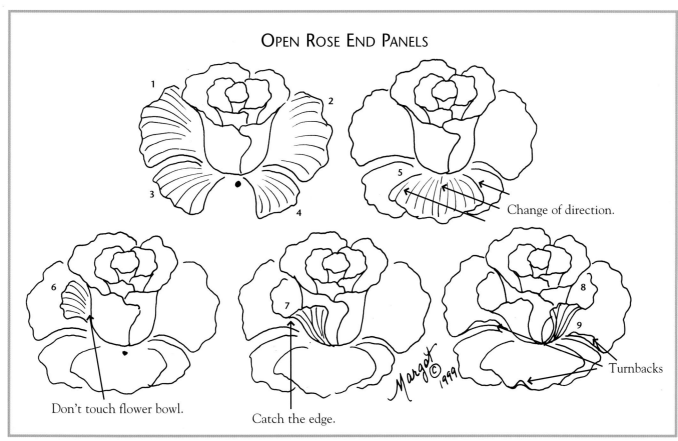

Change of direction.

Don't touch flower bowl.

Catch the edge.

Turnbacks

3 ADD THE NEXT TWO LAYERS

Connect these petals to the last two layers of petals. Your stroke should go in at the waist and out at the hip. Allow these two petals to overlap one another. Dribble, catch and pull each side petal as for the opening bud. Add the front view of the side petals by dribbling partway across the front of the petal, then flare the brush and cut in to the calyx. Continue to catch the dribble and watch for directional changes. For the last stroke, slide in on the chisel edge just before forming the outer edge of the petal. This forms the thin, delicate outer edges of the petals.

THE COMPLETED SIDE PANEL ROSE

THE OPEN ROSES

1 SKIRTED VERSION OF THE OPEN ROSE
Paint three rows of back petals. Connect the inner two rows forming the open bud. Add two more side petals for the skirt. Add the front skirt petals, one overlapping the other. Begin the dribble on the top front petal where it overlaps the bottom petal so the edge of the overlapping petal is lightest.

2 SIDE PETAL COMPLETE
Barely catch the edge of the back row and paint a narrow turnback to form the side petals. Repeat these steps for the second flower on the lid.

3 OPEN ROSE
These roses are on the large side panels on the box and under the lid. Paint three back rows of petals and connect them with the middle of the rose. Remember to go in at the waist and out at the hips! Add the two side skirt petals and three front skirt petals.

4 FRONT VIEW OF SIDE PETALS
Add the front view of the side petals as for the opening rose on the end panel.

THE BACK FACING ROSE

1 PETALS 1,2 AND 3 OF THE BACK FACING ROSE
Load Margot's Multi-load brush with the red mix, pull through Raw Sienna. With the Raw Sienna side of the brush facing up, pull in the darkest petal, marked "1" in the diagram below. For petals 2 and 3 pick up Magnolia White, but do not reload in the other colors. Begin to dribble under petals 4 and 5. Dribble along the outer edge. Turn the white side of the brush to face the outside of the petal, curve the stroke and cut into the calyx.

2 PETALS 4, 5, 6 AND 7
Reload the brush if necessary. Pick up white, repeat the steps for petals 2 and 3. Begin the dribble under petals 6 and 7. Dribble across petal 6, catch and pull to the calyx. Repeat for petal 7.

3 PETAL 8 OF THE BACK FACING ROSE
Dribble across the top of the petal. Turn the white side of the brush to the outside of the petal. Push out on one side and cut to the calyx. Catch the top dribble on the other side. Push the white out and cut into the calyx. Pick up a little more white, facing it up, catch the dribble at the center and pull in to the calyx. Catch and pull in one side beginning to curve the strokes to match the side stroke. Repeat for the other side.

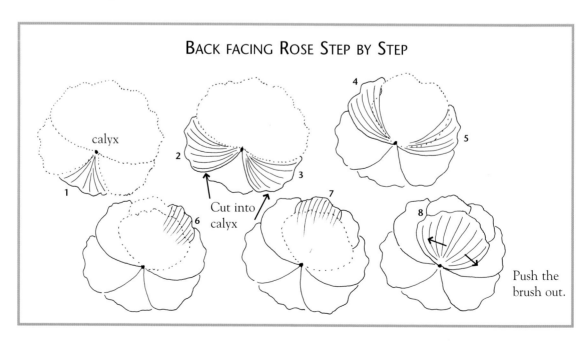

BACK FACING ROSE STEP BY STEP

THE FINISHING TOUCHES

TURNBACKS

With all the flowers painted, check to see if any of them need turnbacks for either correcting a petal or for interest. See the instructions on page 66 for details.

SHADING ON THE FLOWERS

Now is the time to evaluate the flowers to see if any of the petals need to be separated or an area needs darkening. If shading is needed, add a bit more Walnut to the red mix for the shading color. Pick up water in the ½-inch (12mm) angle shader and press off the excess on the side of the water container. Corner load the long hairs with the darkened red mix and stroke back and forth on the wet palette until it looks like you have dirty water on your brush. Then add shading to the flower with the color facing the area to be shaded. Remember you are adding dark shadows not dark paint.

LEAVES BEHIND ROSES

Load the Multi-load brush with Gamal Green, pull through Antique Gold Deep and through Eggshell. Face the light side of the brush toward the top or right of design. Paint one leaf at a time so you have variety throughout. Pull in the center vein beginning at the tip of the leaf. Press, lift and cut, stopping before touching the rose. Keep the light side of the brush facing the light source, push and pull strokes to create the light side of the leaf. Lift off before touching the center vein. Remember that if the strokes are above the curve of the center vein, they will follow the same direction. If they are below the curve, they will change direction. The dark side of the leaf is painted by reloading the dark side in green and the light side in gold over the Eggshell. Pull all leaves behind the roses in this manner.

STEMS AND CALYXES

Load the Multi-load brush as you did for the leaves. Face the light side of the brush up and pull in the stems on all closed and opening buds by applying a little pressure under the bud. Then turn, lift and cut in the stem, turning the brush to face the light source. Pull a stem with even pressure under the open roses where indicated on the pattern. For the back facing rose, apply a little more pressure so the brush opens up to form a larger calyx. Then immediately lift, turn and cut to complete the stem.

THE REMAINING LEAVES

Use the same technique as you did for the leaves behind the roses with the center vein stroke extended to create the stem.

SEPALS

Use the "press, lift, turn and cut strokes." The first two sepal strokes have the light side of the brush facing towards the flower, and for the third stroke face the light side up. These are painted under the opening rosebuds, on either side of the closed buds, and on top of the back facing rose.

THE FINISHING TOUCHES, CONTINUED

TINT THE LEAVES

Make a thin wash of Gamal Green, about 80 percent water and 20 percent color, and paint it over all the leaves. Load the Multi-load brush with thinned color and touch the tip on a paper towel to remove excess paint. This will strengthen the color while allowing all the strokes to show through. Let this dry and repeat for the other leaves. Let this dry and repeat for the largest leaves. This technique helps give value change to the leaves. Wash the brush. Thin some red mix, 90 percent water to 10 percent color, touching the excess color on a paper towel, and add tints to some of the rose leaves for warmth. Let this dry twenty-four hours.

ADD A SOFTENING GLAZE

Make a thin wash of 90 percent water and 10 percent Raw Sienna. Using the 1-inch (25mm) flat wash/glaze brush, apply a thin, even layer of color over all the Raw Linen panels, including the flowers, leaves and background. Allow drying time for each panel. When dry, the color will darken. Repeat if you prefer more softening. Again, let the softening dry thoroughly.

1 THE CRACKLE FINISH
Apply a medium coat of Step 1-Fine Crackle Finish with the 1-inch (25mm) flat wash/glaze brush. Let this dry approximately twenty minutes. Apply a medium coat of Step 2- Fine Crackle Finish and allow to dry overnight. Very fine eggshell cracks will begin to appear as the finish dries. Wash the brush.

2 ANTIQUE THE CRACKLE FINISH
Thin Dark Bronze Metallic to an ink consistency. Work one panel at a time. Brush on the Dark Bronze over the whole panel and immediately wipe off with a soft cloth. This step allows the fine cracks to be accented and further ages the rose design. Let this dry.

3 BLACK BANDS AROUND THE PANELS
The black bands frame each panel and clean up the edges. Tape off a ⅛-inch (0.3cm) band around each panel on the background finish, not the panel itself. Using Margot's Multi-load brush, paint all the bands starting on the tape, so Black paint doesn't end up under the tape. Remove the tape as soon as the band is solid. If some Black accidentally gets under the tape, use your fingernail to remove it before it has a chance to dry. Allow the bands to dry for twenty-four hours before applying varnishes.

4 VARNISHING
Apply four to six coats of gloss varnish to the tortoiseshell areas and four coats of satin varnish to the rest of the box.

5 WAXING
Give the outside of the box a final coat of finishing wax to further enhance the faux finishes.

BOUQUET OF FLOWERS MIRROR

This project is the culmination of all the skills you have learned. You'll enjoy the fancier mums, more intricate tulips, poppies, irises and forget-me-nots, as well as new types of leaves, shadow leaves and lots of tints and washes.

You'll load the brush in a different sequence, like backwards, loading light to dark for the irises.

After you have painted this design and become familiar with the different loads, try using the tulip load for one of the roses in Project 6. Reverse the iris load for a totally different look. Use the poppy load for tulips. Experiment!

Experimenting and coming up with new ways to show flowers is the true beauty of the Contemporary Multi-load Floral Technique. You'll be able to add new flowers to your growing list of contemporary multi-load florals just by looking in the garden.

This pattern may be hand-traced or photocopied for personal use only. Enlarge at 167% to bring it up to full size. Do not transfer the numbers; they are for painting sequence only. Do not transfer the dotted lines; they are to show painting direction.

This pattern may be hand-traced or photocopied for personal use only. Enlarge at 167% to bring it up to full size. Do not transfer the numbers; they are for painting sequence only. Do not transfer the dotted lines; they are to show painting direction.

MATERIALS

PAINT: (D) = DELTA CERAMCOAT ACRYLICS; (DA) = DECOART AMERICANA ACRYLICS

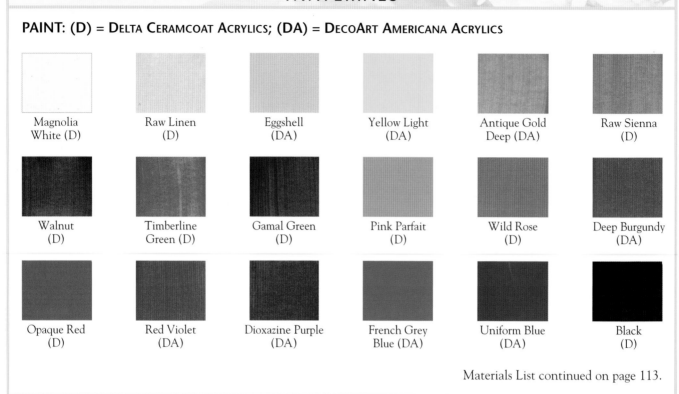

Magnolia White (D)	Raw Linen (D)	Eggshell (DA)	Yellow Light (DA)	Antique Gold Deep (DA)	Raw Sienna (D)
Walnut (D)	Timberline Green (D)	Gamal Green (D)	Pink Parfait (D)	Wild Rose (D)	Deep Burgundy (DA)
Opaque Red (D)	Red Violet (DA)	Dioxazine Purple (DA)	French Grey Blue (DA)	Uniform Blue (DA)	Black (D)

Materials List continued on page 113.

This pattern may be hand-traced or photocopied for personal use only. Enlarge at 200% to bring it up to full size. Do not transfer the numbers; they are for painting sequence only. Do not transfer the dotted lines; they are to show painting direction.

PREPARE THE SURFACE

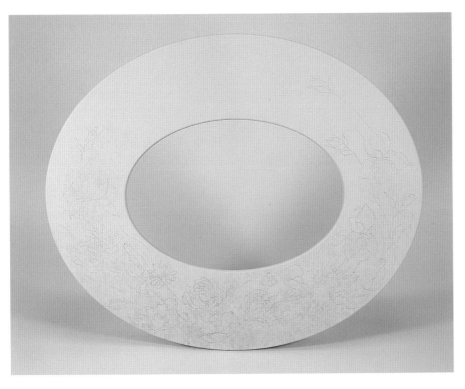

BASECOAT THE MIRROR FRAME
Sand and seal the mirror frame and sand again with a crumpled brown paper bag. Basecoat smoothly and solidly with Raw Linen. Let this dry. Wash the brush. Before transferring the design make a thin wash of Gamal Green. Dampen a silk sponge. Wet the design area with clean water using the 1-inch (25mm) flat wash/glaze brush. Sponge thinned Gamal Green on the background, heaviest at the bottom of the design and fading to nothing at the top. Let dry thoroughly. Transfer the pattern lightly with gray graphite paper. Do not transfer the numbers or dotted lines.

MATERIALS CONT.

SURFACE
- Oval Mirror Frame and Beveled Mirror available from Sechtem's Wood Products

BRUSHES
- Margot's Multi-load
- 1-inch (25mm) flat wash/glaze
- ½-inch (12mm) angle shader

ADDITIONAL SUPPLIES
- Gray graphite paper
- Silk sponge
- Petit-four sponge
- Old toothbrush

PAINT THE STEMS AND LEAVES

1 THE STEMS
Load the Multi-load brush in Gamal Green, pull through Timberline Green and pull through Antique Gold Deep. Pull the thick stems for the poppies and tulips. Pull the stems for the two open mums, but not the back view mums or the mum buds. Reload, picking up a smear of Eggshell and pull the iris stems.

2 MUM AND POPPY LEAVES
Paint the mum leaves using the Multi-load brush loaded with Gamal Green, pulled through Timberline Green, and pulled through Eggshell. Face the light side toward the upper right-hand side. Begin at outer tip of leaf. Touch, lift and cut in for the center vein and stem in one stroke.

Reload the brush with Gamal Green on dark side. Turn the brush over and pull through Timberline Green, and through Antique Gold Deep, then through a smear of Eggshell. Pull in the individual strokes for the light side of the leaf using "press, lift and cut strokes," curving in to the stem. Use the pattern as a guide. Gently wipe off the light side of the brush.

Reload as for the light side, but do not pull through Eggshell. The Antique Gold Deep is the light side of the brush. Face the light side toward the center vein and pull the strokes to fill in the dark side of the leaf.

Reload just the light side of the brush in Timberline Green, Antique Gold Deep and Eggshell and re-stroke any of the leaves that need to be lighter at the outer edge.

Use the same brush loads for the poppy leaves, but make the edges more uneven and shaggy. Pull the poppy and mum leaves barely extending onto the petal design. Use the "press, lift and cut strokes." For the light side of the leaf, load the brush with Gamal Green, pull through Timberline Green, pull through Antique Gold Deep, pull through a smear of Eggshell. Leave off Eggshell for the dark side of the leaf.

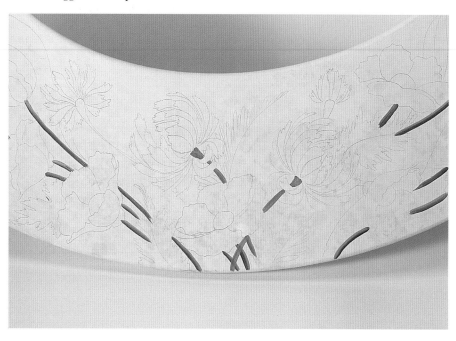

PAINT THE MUMS

1 MUM—BACK VIEW AND BUDS
Load the Multi-load brush in the red mix (see page 30 for mixing instructions), pull through Raw Sienna, pick up Magnolia White. All the petals are "dribble, catch and pull" to calyx. Study the diagram on page 112 to see the different layers of petals. Start with the petals furthest back and keep picking up white on your brush, so the petals at the front of the flower are the lightest. Refer to the pattern as you paint some of the design, but remember it is just a guide. Wash the brush.

2 STEMS FOR BACK VIEWS AND BUDS
Reload the Multi-load brush with Gamal Green, Timberline Green, Antique Gold Deep and a smear of Eggshell. Keep Eggshell facing up and pull in the calyxes and stems for the back views and buds with the "press, lift, turn and cut stroke."

3 OPEN MUMS
These open mums are painted just like the back views, again starting farthest back and working towards the front. They differ from the mums in Project 1 by being much looser in design and not quite so neat.

PAINT THE POPPIES AND IRIS LEAVES

1 THE FIRST POPPY PETAL
Load the Multi-load brush with Wild Rose, pull through Deep Burgundy. Turn the brush over and pull through the Pink Parfait on top of the Wild Rose and pick up Magnolia White on Pink Parfait. Begin with petal 1 shown in the diagram on page 112. With the white facing up, dribble, catch and pull to the calyx.

2 SECOND POPPY PETAL
Start on the left, dribble across the top of the first petal. Push the white out and over the first petal. With the white side of the brush facing up, catch and pull the strokes to fill the petal. Watch for any direction changes on this petal.

3 THIRD POPPY PETAL
Begin the dribble at the left. Flare the bristles out onto petal 2, and cut in to calyx. Catch and pull the strokes to fill the petal. Wash the brush.

4 TURNBACKS

Turnbacks are done before this flower is complete. Flatten the brush in Deep Burgundy on the dark side, pick up a little white. Begin at the outer edge of the petal, with the white side of the brush facing the inside of the petal. Touch, lift, push white towards the inner petal. Release the pressure, lift, and cut to the calyx. Look for turnbacks on the outer edges of the outer petals, referring to the pattern on page 112 for placement.

5 BACK PETALS ON ALL SIDE-VIEW POPPIES COMPLETE

Paint the back petals for the other two side-view poppies following the pattern's numerical order. Paint the centers on these views before the front petals. When painting the iris leaves, jump over the petals that will overlap the leaves. On a light background, the leaf would show through the flower. Remember not to turn the brush: just push, release, lift to the tip and push, release, pushing in the other direction, lift to the tip and push, release, changing direction once again. Some of the larger iris leaves are done with two strokes side by side—light side of brush facing outer edge of leaf. Before painting more flowers, pull in the iris leaves using the leaf/ribbon stroke. Load in Gamal Green, pull through Timberline Green, pull through Antique Gold Deep, pick up Magnolia White. Face white to light source.

Poppy Centers and Front Petals

1 THE POPPY CENTERS
The centers are painted wet-in-wet. Pick up a good bit of Black on the Multi-load brush and tap in the center unevenly. Extend a little out past the pattern to create the center.

2 TAP IN THE LIGHT AREAS
Wipe the brush. Pick up Antique Gold Deep and tap in the top two-thirds of the center. Stay away from the extra Black outside the pattern. Fade at the bottom into the Black. Wipe the brush and pick up Magnolia White. Tap in the top one-third of the center on top of the Gold, fading into the Gold at the bottom.

3 PAINT THE BLACK LINES
Wipe the brush. Really flatten on both sides of the brush in black. Use the knife edge to connect with the extra black outside the center and cut a few lines that follow the lines of paint already created on the petals. These lines suggest the dark areas on the petals and give some variety to the poppies.

4 BLACK LINEWORK COMPLETED

Pull in the black lines unevenly in both length and width until the outline of the center is gone. Repeat for the other poppies. Roll the brush to a point and load the tip of the brush in Black. Tap in dots on top of and slightly beyond the black lines. Wash the brush. Repeat with Antique Gold Deep. Wash the brush.

5 FRONT SIDE PETALS ON POPPY

Load the Multi-load brush as you did on page 116. Start the dribble at outer edge of the flower with the white of the brush facing the top edge of the petal. Come up over the center, flare the bristles and cut into the calyx. Pull across the dribble only far enough to reach the outer edge of the pattern. For the last stroke, barely catch the dribble. The tip of the brush should actually be in the paint, not touching the surface. Slide over, then down the side, blending the outer edge of the petal. Repeat for the other side. Wash the brush.

6 TO COMPLETE THE POPPIES

Add calyxes by multi-loading the brush with Gamal Green, Timberline Green, Antique Gold Deep and a smear of Eggshell. Hold the brush parallel to the flower bottom with the light side facing away from the flower. Connect the brush under the flower and apply pressure, pushing out the light side. Release to the tip. Dribble across the top of the front petal. Turn the Eggshell down and pull in the middle stroke. For the poppy bud, paint the middle back petal with Wild Rose, Deep Burgundy, and Pink Parfait. Then pick up Magnolia White for the rest of the petals.

THE TULIPS

1 PAINT CLOSED TULIP AND BEGIN OPENING TULIP
All strokes are "dribble, catch and pull." Follow the numbered sequence on the diagram on page 121. Multi-load in Antique Gold Deep, pull through Red Violet, turn the brush over and pull through Yellow Light and pick up Magnolia White on the Yellow Light side. Pick up Magnolia White as you work towards the front of the flower. Load the brush the same for all tulips. Watch the direction of the flower petals. Be aware of where the calyx is.

2 OPENING TULIP RIGHT SIDE
Even though this tulip has only five petals, I have broken it down. It is easier to control the direction and makes it resemble a Parrot tulip. Reload white for each step.

3 OPENING TULIP COMPLETE
Finish the left side following the previous steps. When you dribble the white, tuck petal 11 in around petal 5. Remember, the pattern is a guide.

4 ALL TULIPS PAINTED
The last version of these tulips is the open tulip. Study the diagram on page 122 for the numbered sequence for painting. Pick up white each time after petal one. Do not dribble for these petals. Pull the strokes in with the gold side of the brush facing up. This flower looks like the closed tulip with extra petals falling away. Remember to pull to the calyx.

TULIPS STEP BY STEP

CLOSED TULIP

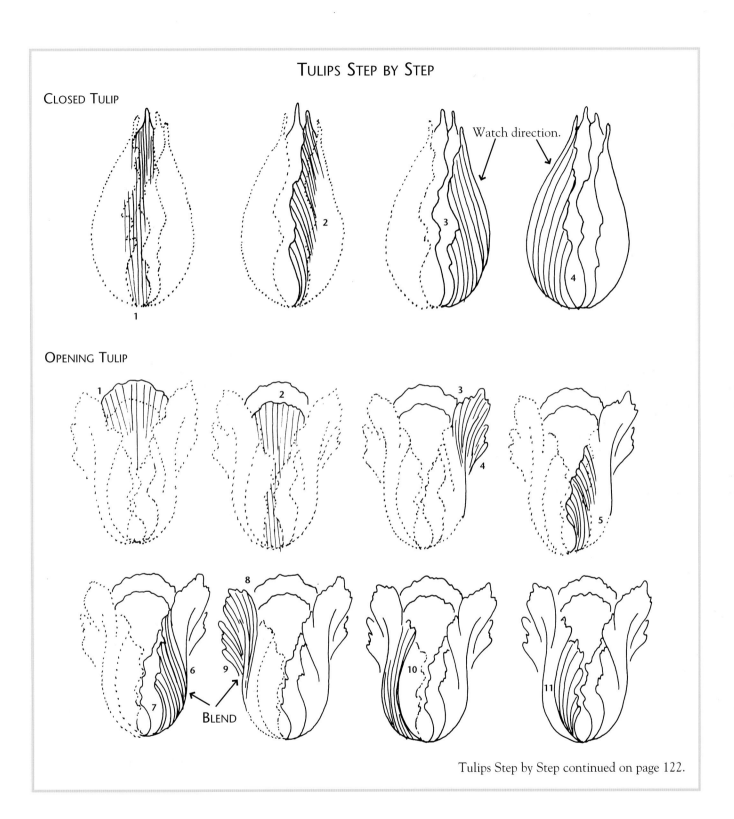

Watch direction.

OPENING TULIP

BLEND

Tulips Step by Step continued on page 122.

OPEN TULIP

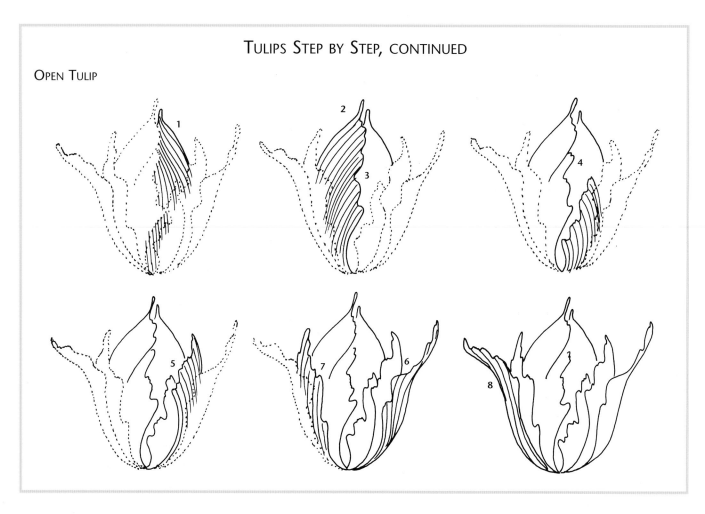

IRISES STEP BY STEP

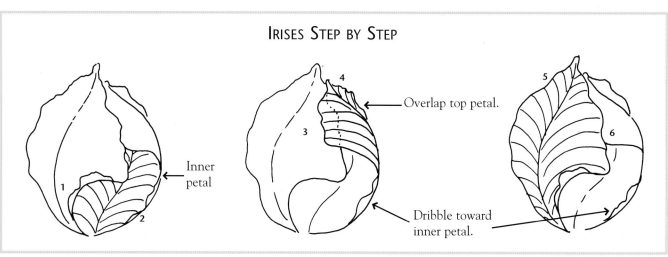

Inner petal

Overlap top petal.

Dribble toward inner petal.

THE IRISES

1 BEGIN THE RED-VIOLET IRIS
Load in Magnolia White, pull through Antique Gold Deep, and pick up Red Violet. Dribble along the top of the petal. Remove the excess Red Violet. Barely catch the dribble and pull towards the middle of the petal that connects to the calyx. Follow the numerical sequence on pattern. For the one Red-Violet iris, load in Magnolia White on a clean brush. Pull through a smear of Antique Gold Deep, but not too much. Pick up Red Violet on the gold side. Dribble and wipe off the excess Red Violet from your brush. Just barely catch the Red Violet so streaks of color get pulled with the white. If the white begins to get too violet, wash the brush and reload.

2 ADD MORE PETALS
As petals are added, the shape and flow of the flower appears. Wash the brush and reload as necessary to keep the white clean.

3 IRIS BEARDS
Load in Antique Gold Deep, and pick up white. Face the white side of the brush toward the top of the flower. Tap in the beard beginning at the back of the petal, staying on the center of the petal and curving with the center vein. Refer to the diagram on page 122 for placement.

4 IRIS BUDS
Load in Magnolia White, pull through a little Antique Gold Deep and pick up Dioxazine Purple. Remove the excess Dioxazine Purple. Wash and reload the brush to keep the white fresh. Follow the numerical sequence watching the directional changes. Paint the buds with the same load. "Dribble, catch and pull" following the numerical sequence. Paint the sepals in leaf colors using "press, lift, turn and cut" strokes, facing the white up. Refresh white where one sepal overlaps another.

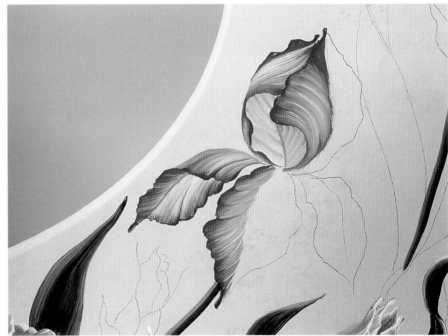

THE FILLER FLOWERS

FILLER FORGET-ME-NOTS AND LEAVES

Paint freehand forget-me-nots with small leaves, where they are needed. Place them in groups, but once in a while tuck one in alone. Refer to the photo on page 108 for placement. Do not place any flowers on the top half of the frame. Load in Uniform Blue and pull through Magnolia White for the flowers at the bottom of the design. Midway to the top of the design, change the load to French Grey Blue and pull through white. The petal stroke is a quick press-and-lift stroke. For the centers, wash the brush and load in Deep Burgundy and pick up Antique Gold Deep. Face the Gold side toward the right, press and lift. Reload as necessary. Wash the brush. For the leaves, using the flattened multi-load brush loaded with Gamal Green, start on the chisel, pull and return to the chisel. Use the same growth pattern as the larger leaves.

THE FINISHING TOUCHES

1 ADD TINTS
Add dirty water tints of Deep Burgundy to the Purple Iris, tints of Dioxazine Purple to the edges of some of the poppies. Shade the mums, where needed, with thinned Walnut. Wash the brush. Cover the flowers and spatter the whole frame with an old toothbrush and thinned Gamal Green toned down with the red mix from page 30. Remove the cover and spatter the flowers. Use a small flat sponge and full-strength Gamal Green to paint the inner and outer edges of the frame.

2 FILLER LEAVES AND STEMS
Using the Multi-load brush and straight Gamal Green, make small chisel-edge strokes to form the leaves. Begin on the chisel edge, pull across and end on the chisel-edge. When pulling free-hand leaves, remember to connect them with the stem. Paint the stems anywhere you like, with the knife edge of the brush loaded in Gamal Green. Wash the brush.

3 ERASE GRAPHITE
Erase all graphite lines. If they are caught under the wash in the next step, they will be permanent.

4 SHADING BEHIND THE FLOWERS
Thin Gamal Green with water. Using the ½-inch (12mm) angle shader, float thinned color behind the flowers. Then tap into the wet color with your finger, to keep the color soft. Shade darker at the bottom and fade to nothing at the top of the design.

5 THE SHADOW LEAVES
Using the multi-load brush, pull in shadow leaves (as indicated on the pattern with dotted lines) with very thin Gamal Green. Start on the chisel, pull and return to the chisel. Do not reload until there is no color left in the brush. Shade the poppies where the petals overlap with thinned Gamal Green and the ½-inch (12mm) angle shader. Shade the mums if needed with thinned Walnut.

6 VARNISHING AND WAXING
Let the mirror dry twenty-four hours. Varnish with four to six coats of spray satin varnish. Let this dry and apply a coat of Finishing Wax.

PATTERN FOR COVER ART

This pattern may be hand-traced or photocopied for personal use only. Enlarge at 145% to bring it up to full size. Do not transfer the dotted lines. They are to show painting direction and shadow leaves.

List of Suppliers

Surfaces

Wooden Door Guards
Jim Bittner
9370 W. Emerald Oaks Dr.
Crystal River, FL 34428
(352)563-6349

Glass Corner Panel 2018S
Cooper's Works
1360 Berryman Ave.
Library, PA 15129
(412)835-2441

Oval Frame and Mirror OMF-1
Jacobean Table JT-1
Sechtem's Wood Products
533 E. Margaret St.
Russell, KS 67665
(800)255-4285
(785)483-2912

Sewing Box
Valhalla Designs
343 Twin Pines Dr.
Glendale, OR 97442
(541)832-3260

Memory Album Cover #3703
Walnut Hollow
1409 State Road 23
Dodgeville, WI 53533-2112
(608)935-2341

Small Oval Box #OB973
Woodcrafts
P.O. Box 78
Bicknell, IN 47512
(812)735-4829
(800)733-4820

Products

Etching Liquid
B&B Products, Inc.
18700 N. 107th Ave., Suite 13
Sun City, AZ 85373
(888)382-4255
(602)933-2962

Real Liquid Metals, Patinas
and Rusts
Chemtek, Inc.
11527 S.E. Highway 212
Clackamas, OR 97015
(888)871-8100
(503)631-7523

Americana Bottled Acrylic Paint
DecoArt
P.O. Box 386
Stanford, KY 40484
(606)365-3193

Ceramcoat Bottled Acrylic Paint
Delta Technical Coatings, Inc.
2550 Pellissier Pl.
Whittier, CA 90601
(562)695-7969

Brushes
Eagle Brush, Inc.
431 Commerce Park Dr. SE
Suite 100 & 101
Marietta, GA 30060
(770)419-4855
(800)832-4532

Prepping and Finishing Products
J.W. Etc.
2205 First St., Suite 103
Simi Valley, California 93065
(805)526-5066

Sta-Wet Palette
Masterson Art Products
P.O. Box 10775
Glendale, Arizona 85318
800-965-2675

INDEX